Guard Dog

Philip Wooderson

Illustrated by Dave Burroughs

A & C Black · London

Chapter One

I didn't want to go to the market, but Dad saw this as his chance to stop me playing GUARD DOG all the rest of Saturday morning.

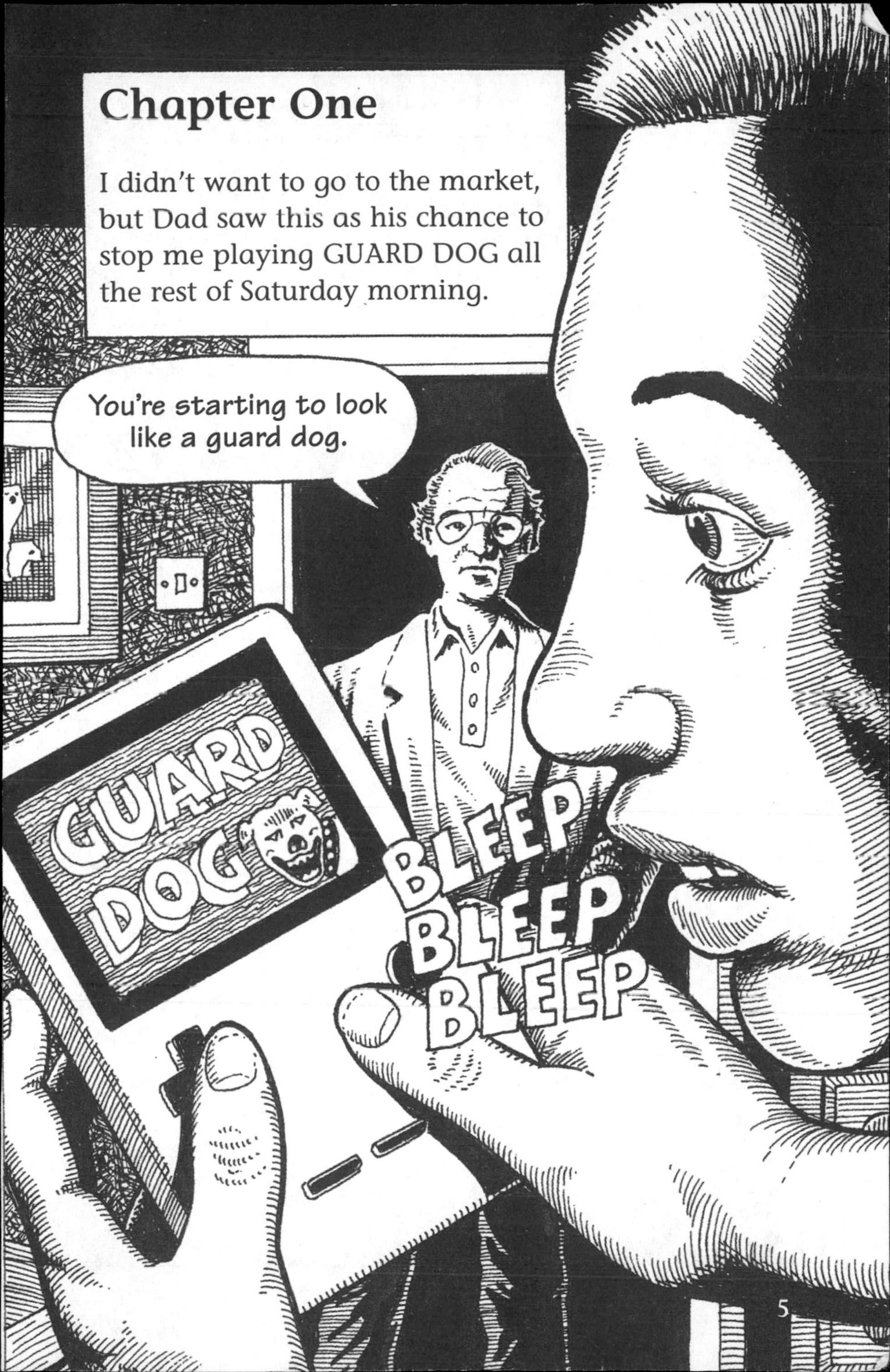
You're starting to look like a guard dog.
GUARD DOG
BLEEP
BLEEP
BLEEP

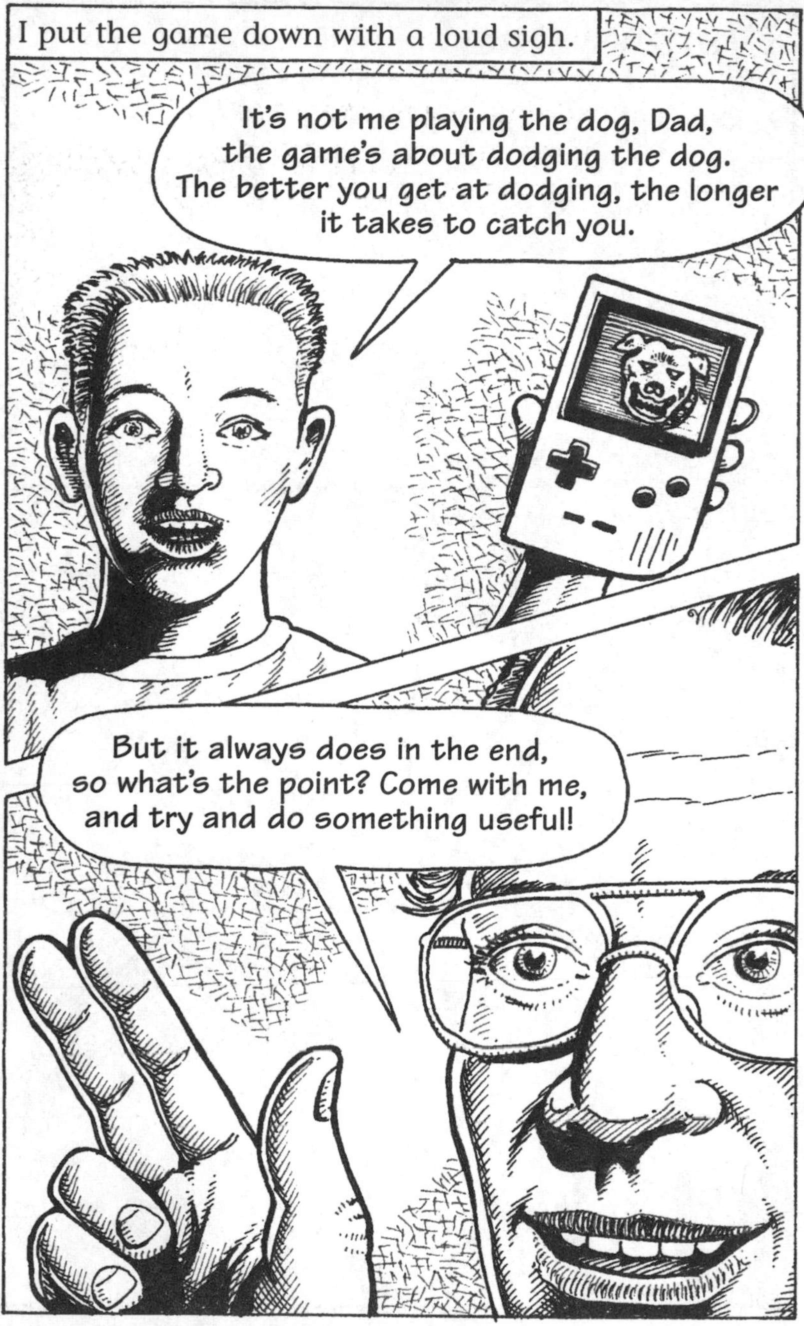
I put the game down with a loud sigh.
It's not me playing the dog, Dad, the game's about dodging the dog. The better you get at dodging, the longer it takes to catch you.
But it always does in the end, so what's the point? Come with me, and try and do something useful!

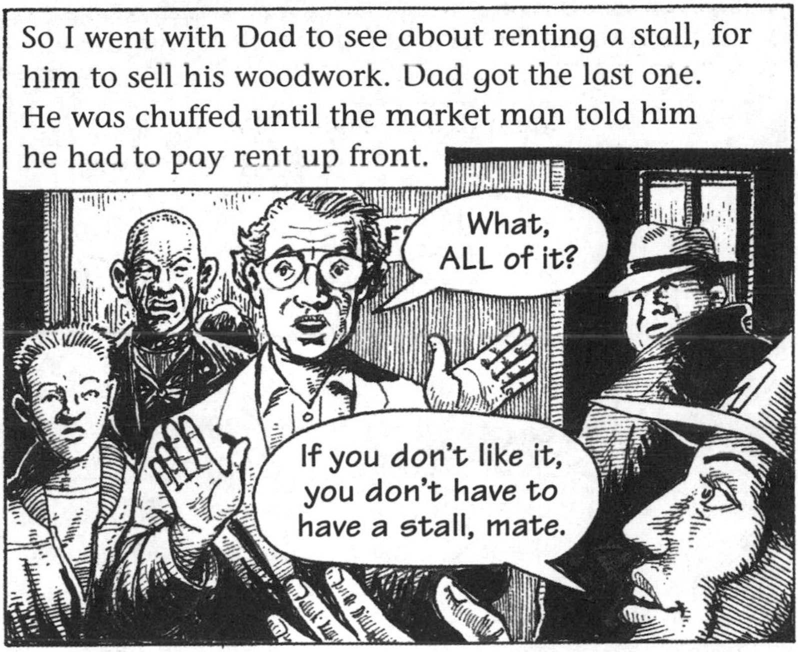
So I went with Dad to see about renting a stall, for him to sell his woodwork. Dad got the last one. He was chuffed until the market man told him he had to pay rent up front.
What, ALL of it?
If you don't like it, you don't have to have a stall, mate.

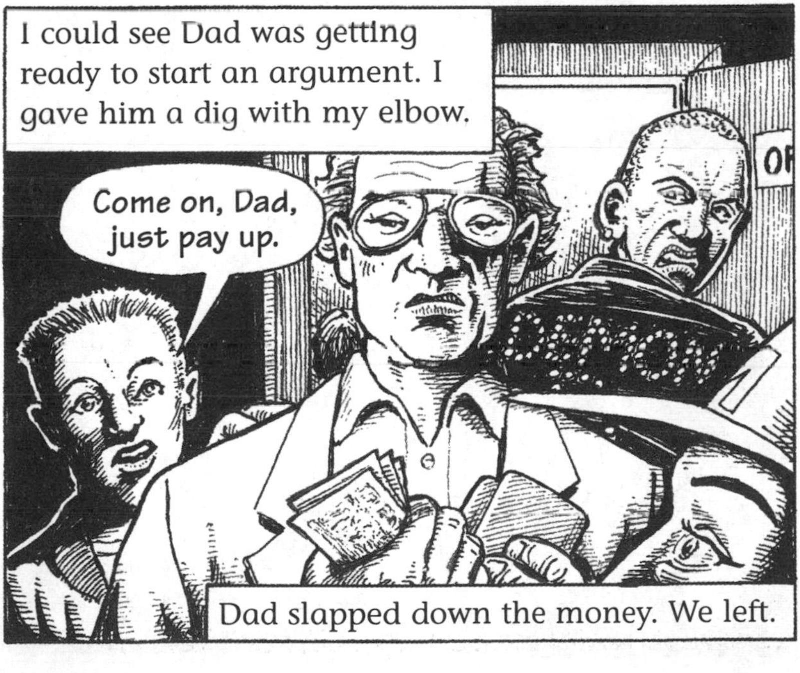
I could see Dad was getting ready to start an argument. I gave him a dig with my elbow.
Come on, Dad, just pay up.
Dad slapped down the money. We left.

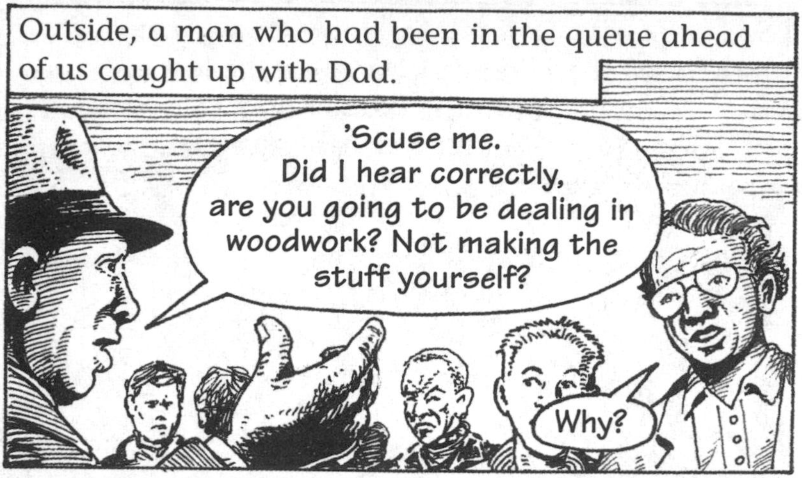
Outside, a man who had been in the queue ahead of us caught up with Dad.
'Scuse me. Did I hear correctly, are you going to be dealing in woodwork? Not making the stuff yourself?
Why?

Dad had been working like fury, every evening for weeks turning out wooden lampstands, salad bowls, spoons and door-stops.

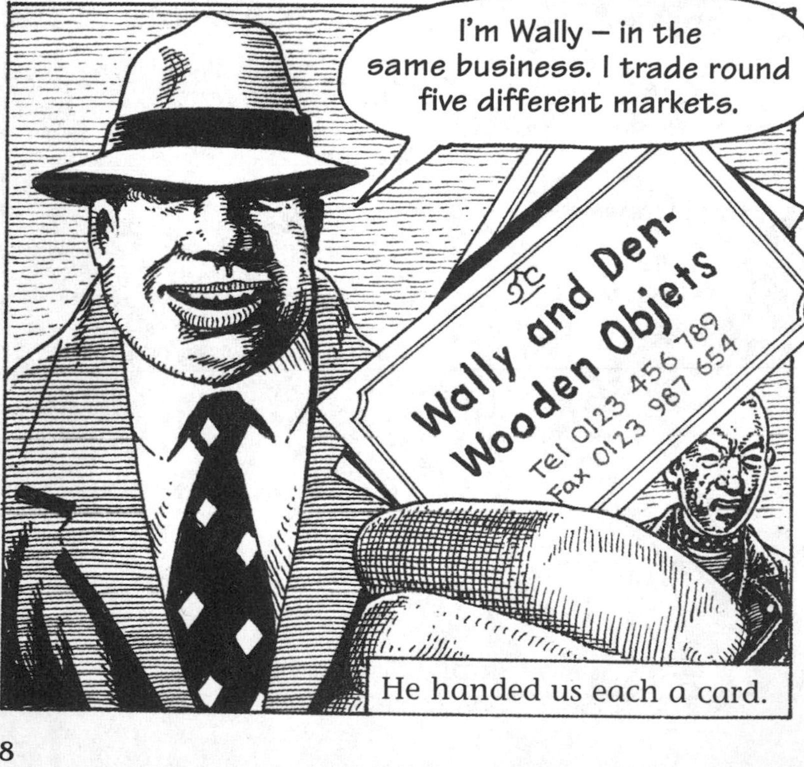
I'm Wally – in the same business. I trade round five different markets.
Wally and Den-
Wooden Objets
Tel 0123 456 789
Fax 0123 987 654
He handed us each a card.

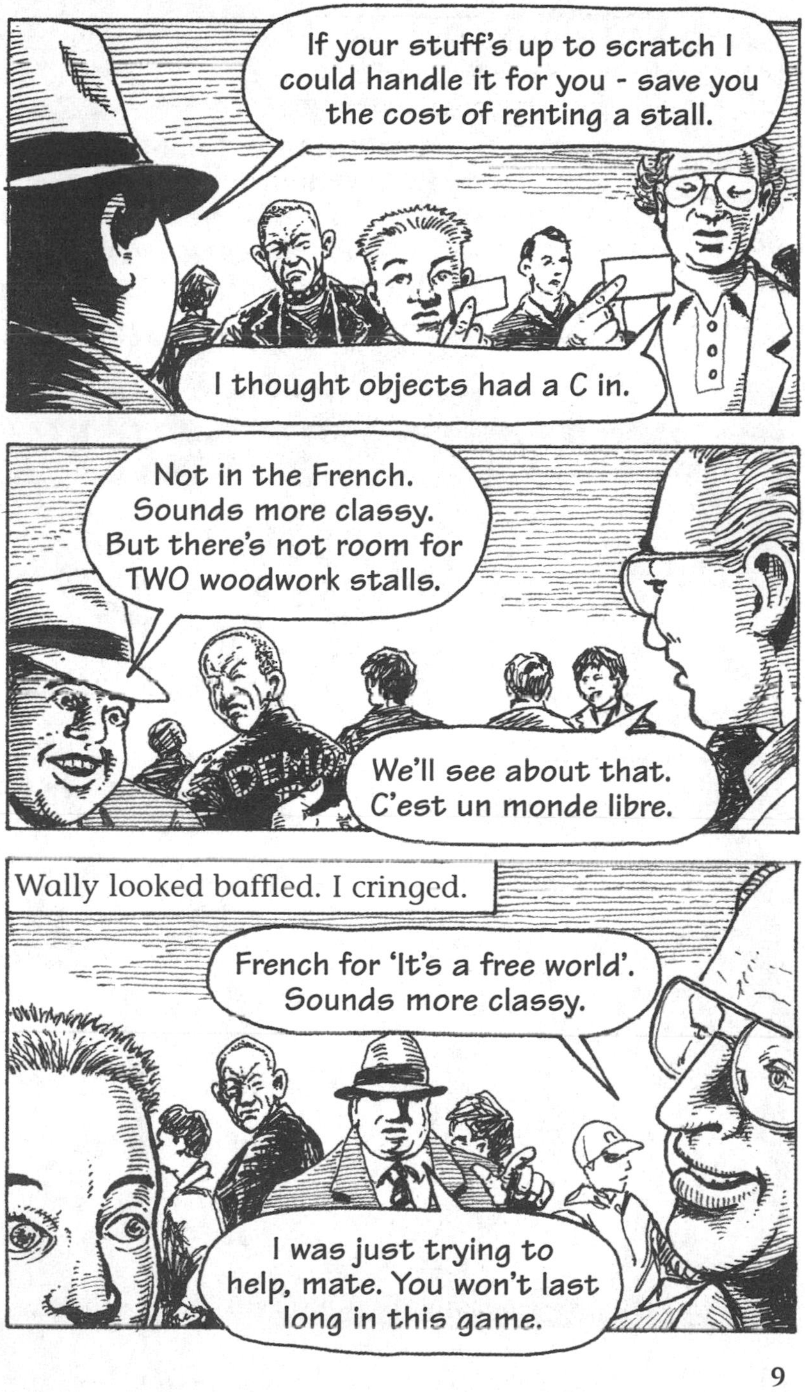
If your stuff's up to scratch I could handle it for you - save you the cost of renting a stall.
I thought objects had a C in.
Not in the French. Sounds more classy. But there's not room for TWO woodwork stalls.
We'll see about that. C'est un monde libre.
Wally looked baffled. I cringed.
French for 'It's a free world'. Sounds more classy.
I was just trying to help, mate. You won't last long in this game.

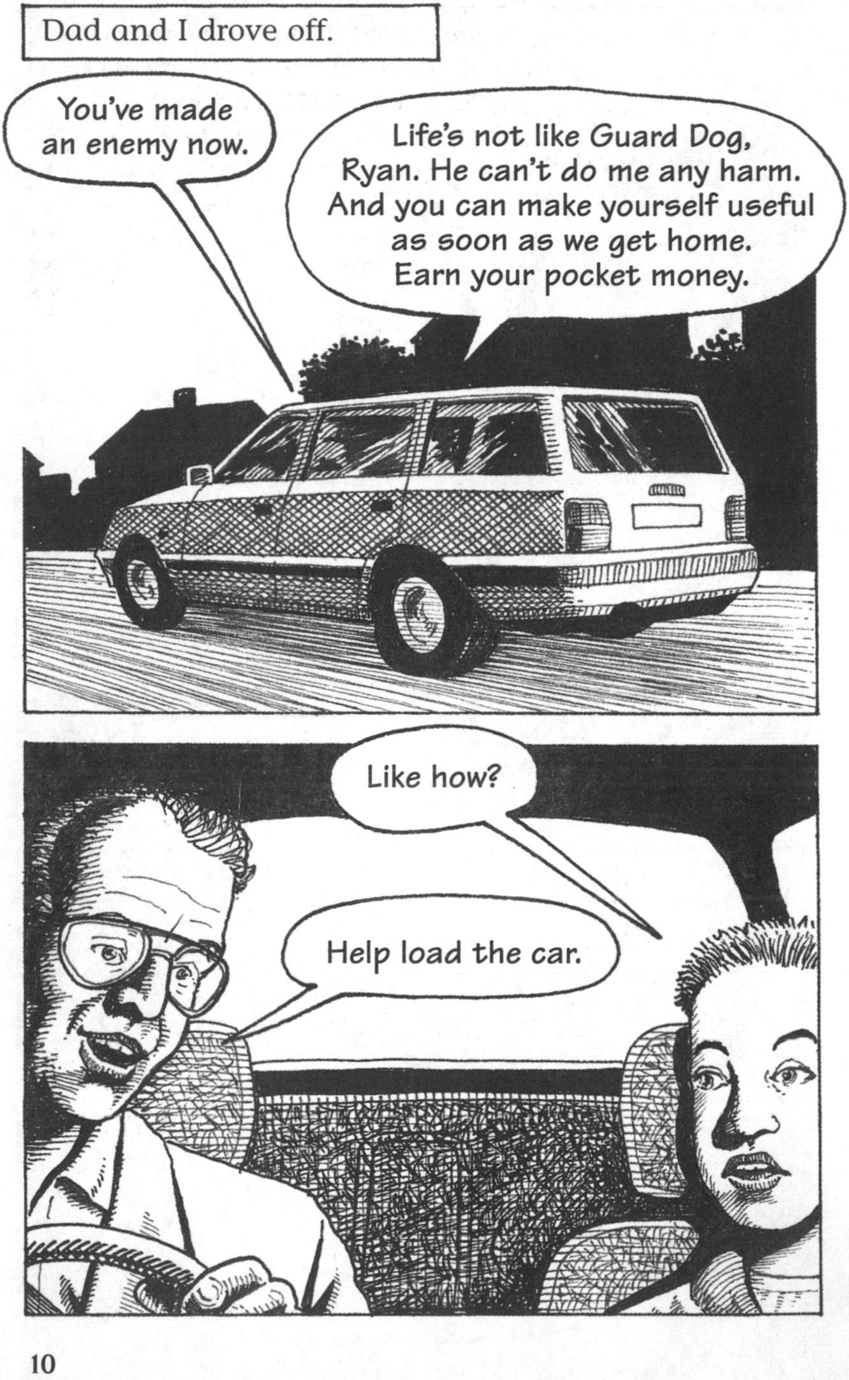
Dad and I drove off.
You've made an enemy now.
Life's not like Guard Dog, Ryan. He can't do me any harm. And you can make yourself useful as soon as we get home. Earn your pocket money.
Like how?
Help load the car.

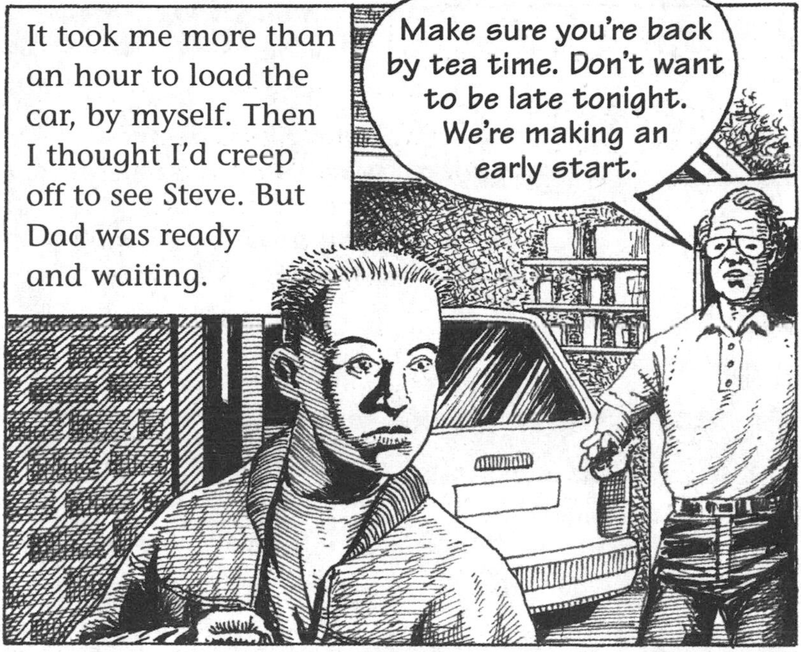
It took me more than an hour to load the car, by myself. Then I thought I'd creep off to see Steve. But Dad was ready and waiting.
Make sure you're back by tea time. Don't want to be late tonight. We're making an early start.

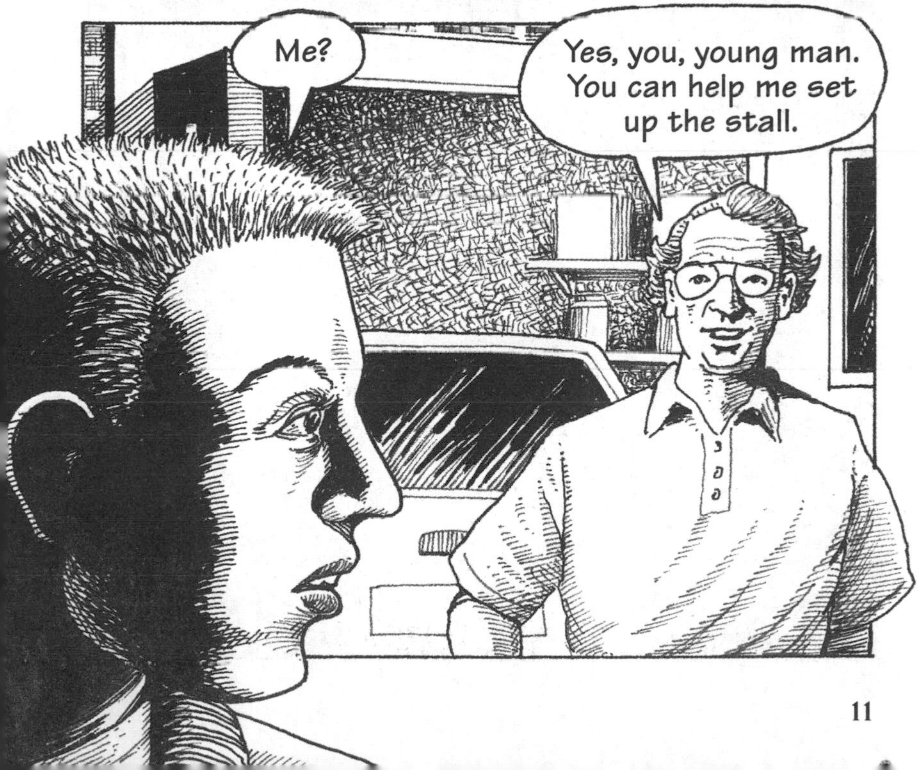
Me?
Yes, you, young man. You can help me set up the stall.

Chapter Two

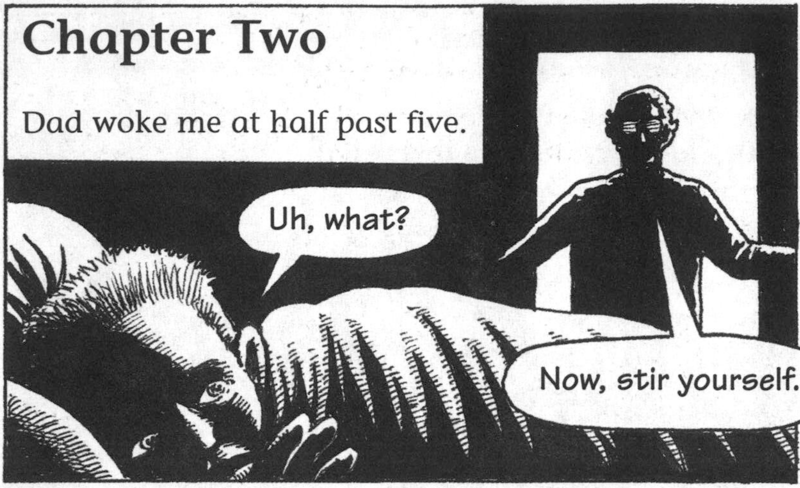
Dad woke me at half past five.
Uh, what?
Now, stir yourself.

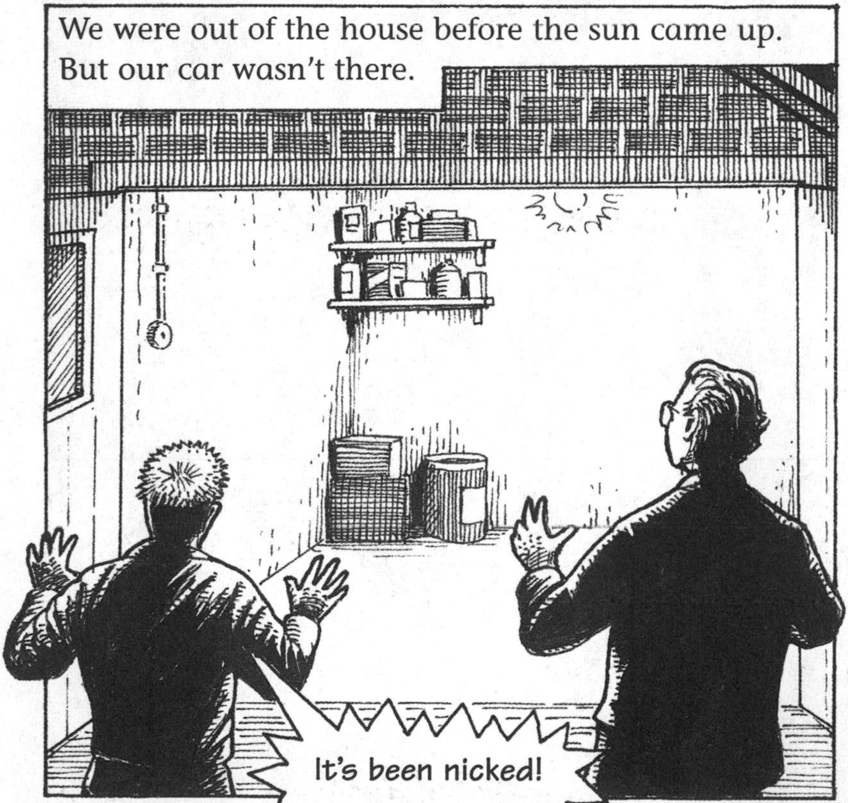
We were out of the house before the sun came up.
But our car wasn't there.
It's been nicked!

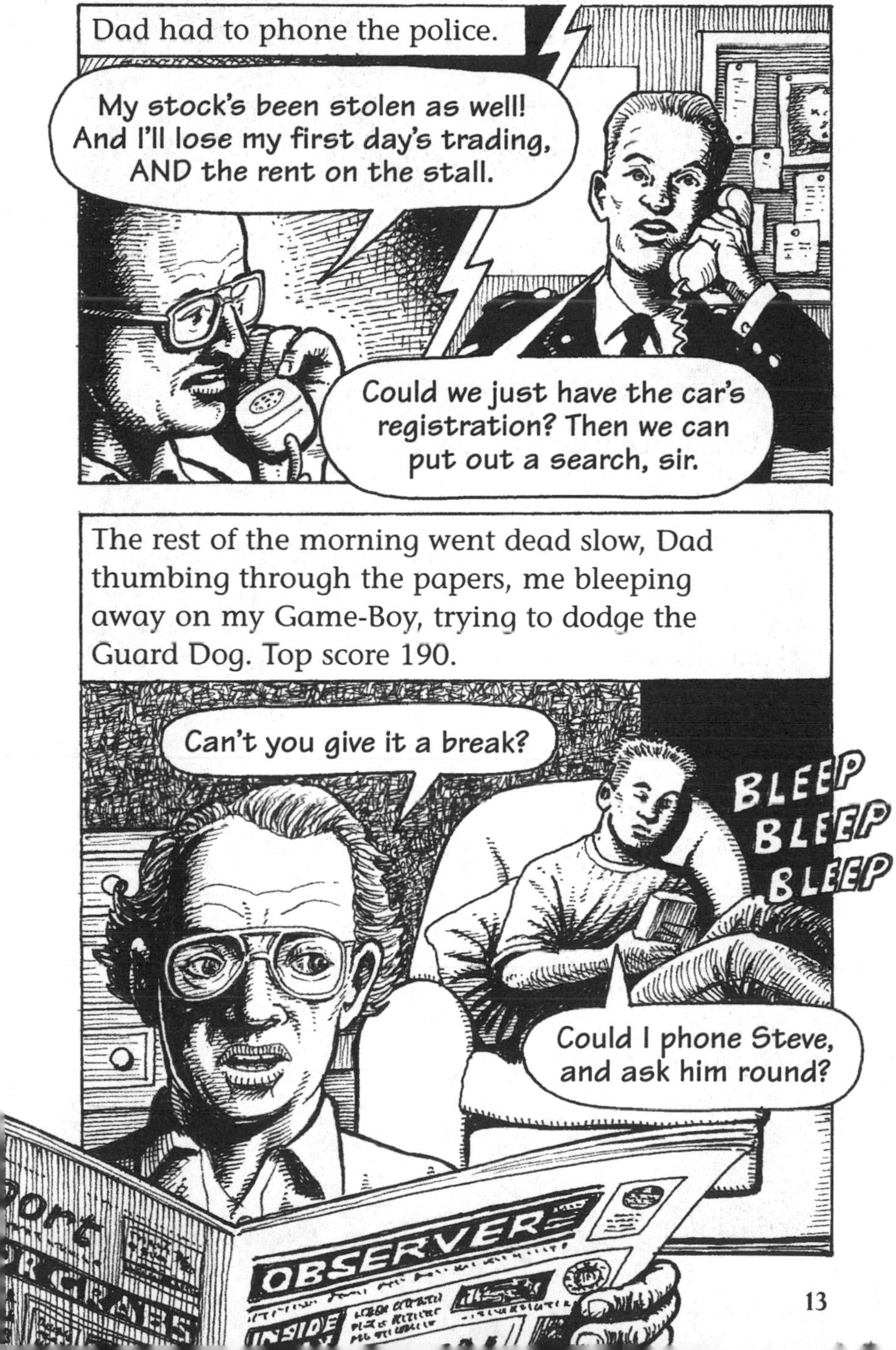
Dad had to phone the police.
My stock's been stolen as well! And I'll lose my first day's trading, AND the rent on the stall.
Could we just have the car's registration? Then we can put out a search, sir.
The rest of the morning went dead slow, Dad thumbing through the papers, me bleeping away on my Game-Boy, trying to dodge the Guard Dog. Top score 190.
Can't you give it a break?
BLEEP
BLEEP
BLEEP
Could I phone Steve, and ask him round?
OBSERVER

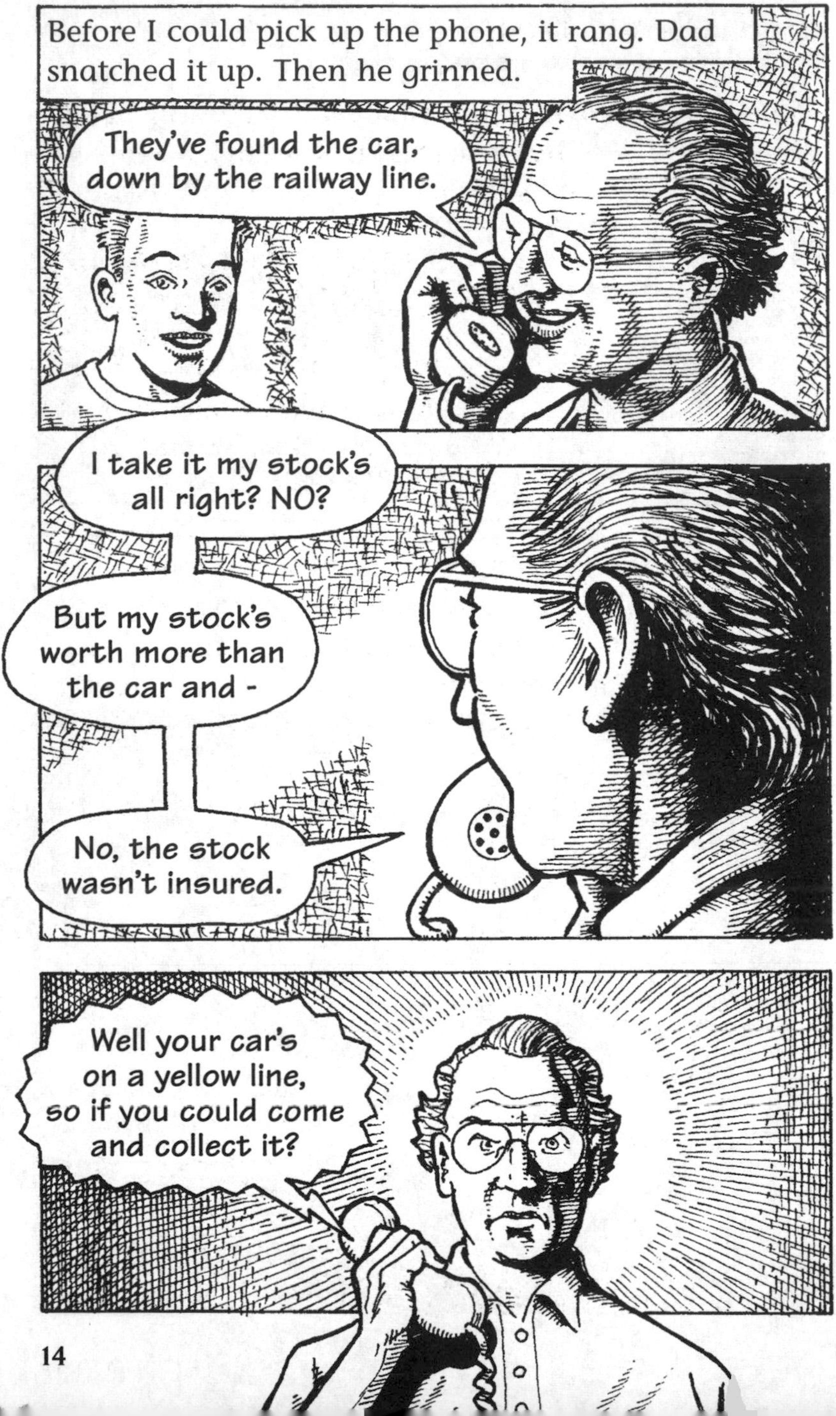
Before I could pick up the phone, it rang. Dad snatched it up. Then he grinned.
They've found the car, down by the railway line.
I take it my stock's all right? NO?
But my stock's worth more than the car and -
No, the stock wasn't insured.
Well your car's on a yellow line, so if you could come and collect it?

Chapter Three

We found the car in a grimy street, by the railway arches. The thief had smashed a window and hot-wired the ignition. And there was a parking ticket on the windscreen already.

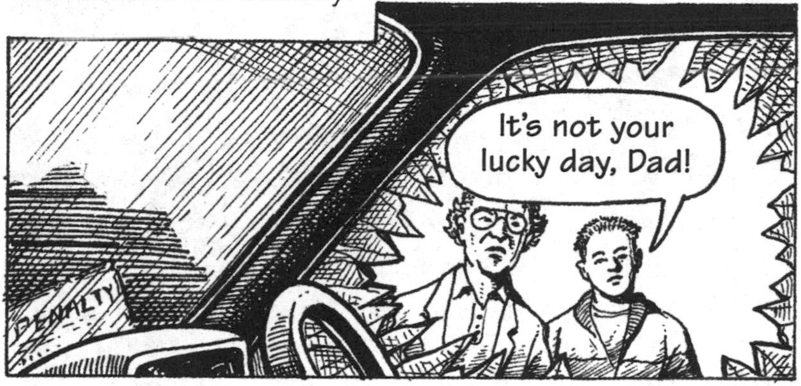
PENALTY
It's not your lucky day, Dad!

Then we cruised round the town for an hour, Dad stopping to search every skip, but we didn't find one single lampstand.

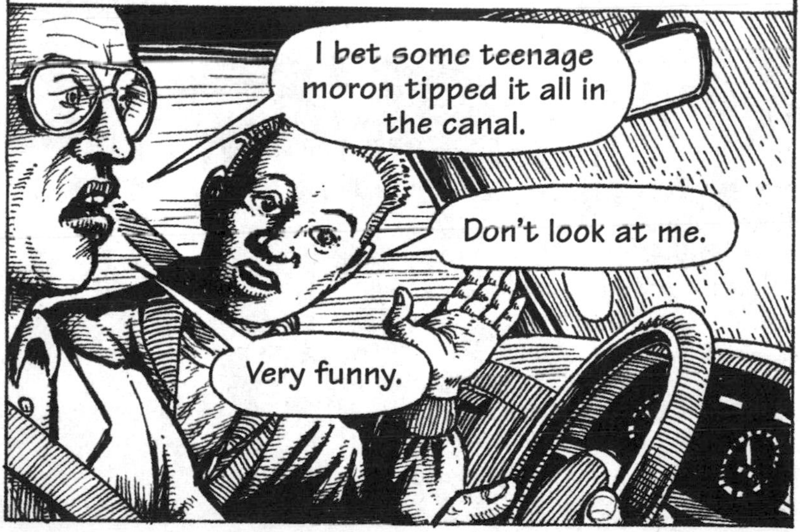
I bet some teenage moron tipped it all in the canal.
Don't look at me.
Very funny.

As soon as we got home, Dad phoned the market office to tell them why we weren't there.

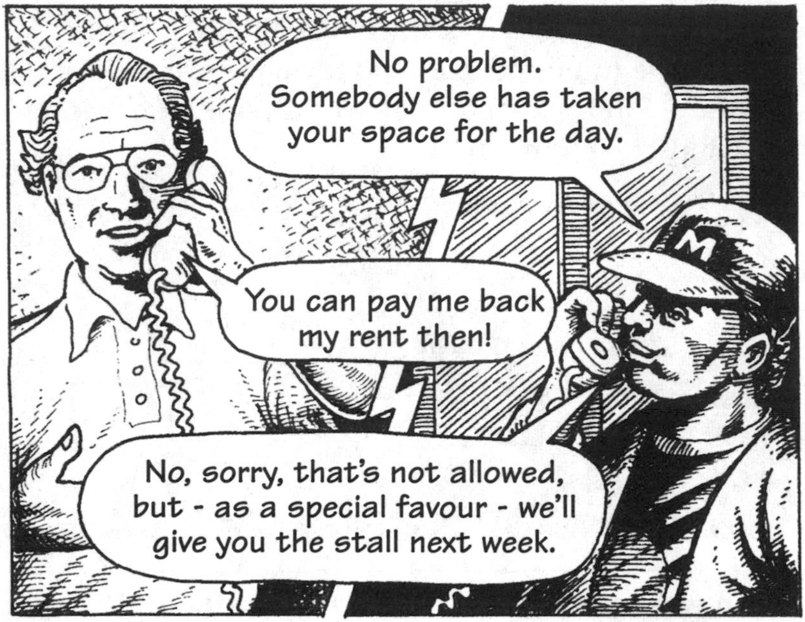
No problem. Somebody else has taken your space for the day.
You can pay me back my rent then!
No, sorry, that's not allowed, but - as a special favour - we'll give you the stall next week.

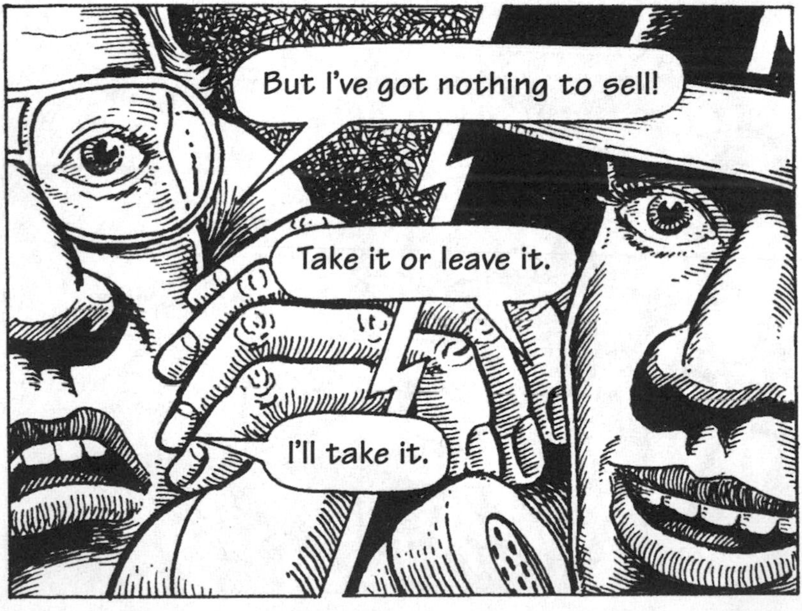
But I've got nothing to sell!
Take it or leave it.
I'll take it.

Dad cheered up after this. He went off to the timber yard to buy himself some more wood, and when he came home he got busy, shut up in his garden shed. He didn't ask me to help, and after a couple of hours bleeping away at Guard Dog, best score 203, I was bored out of my brain.

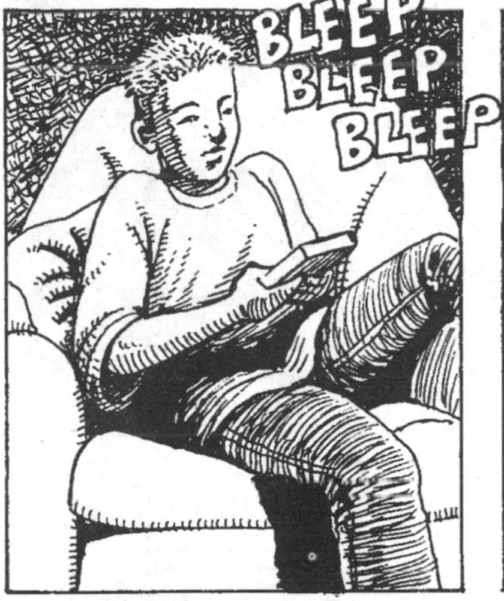
BLEEP
BLEEP
BLEEP

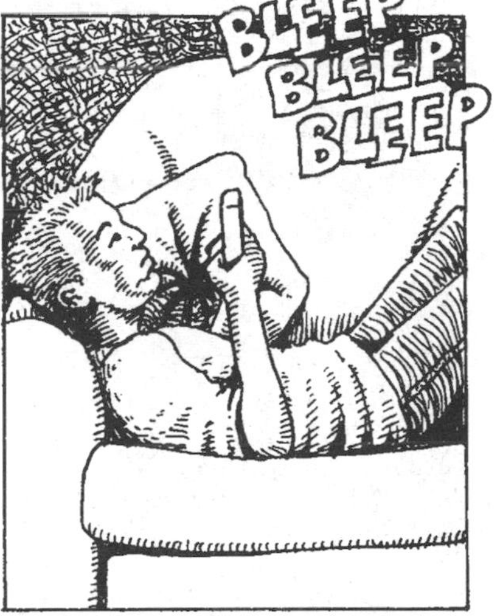
BLEEP
BLEEP
BLEEP

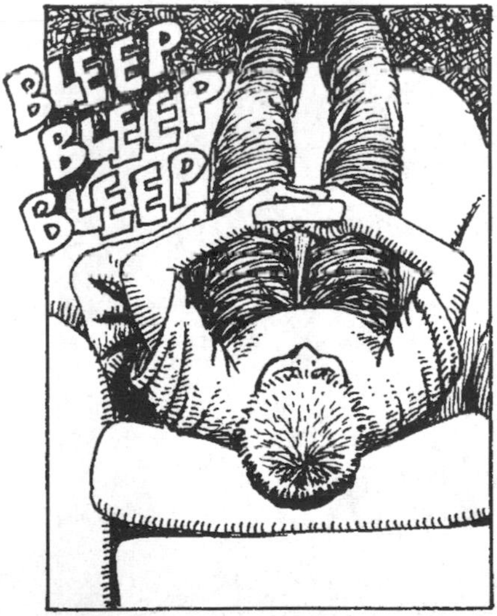
BLEEP
BLEEP
BLEEP

I decided to I slip off to Steve's house.

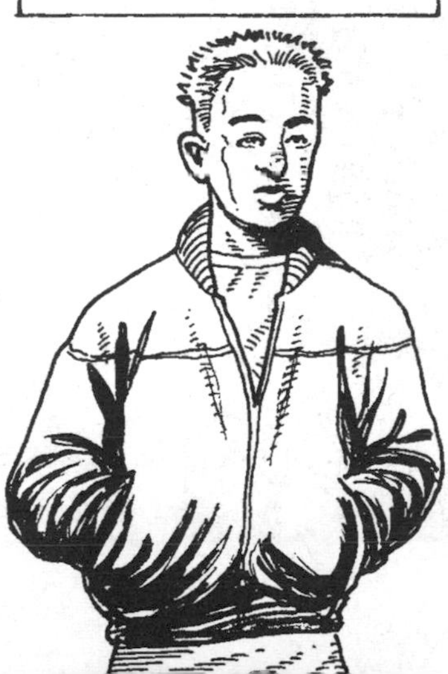

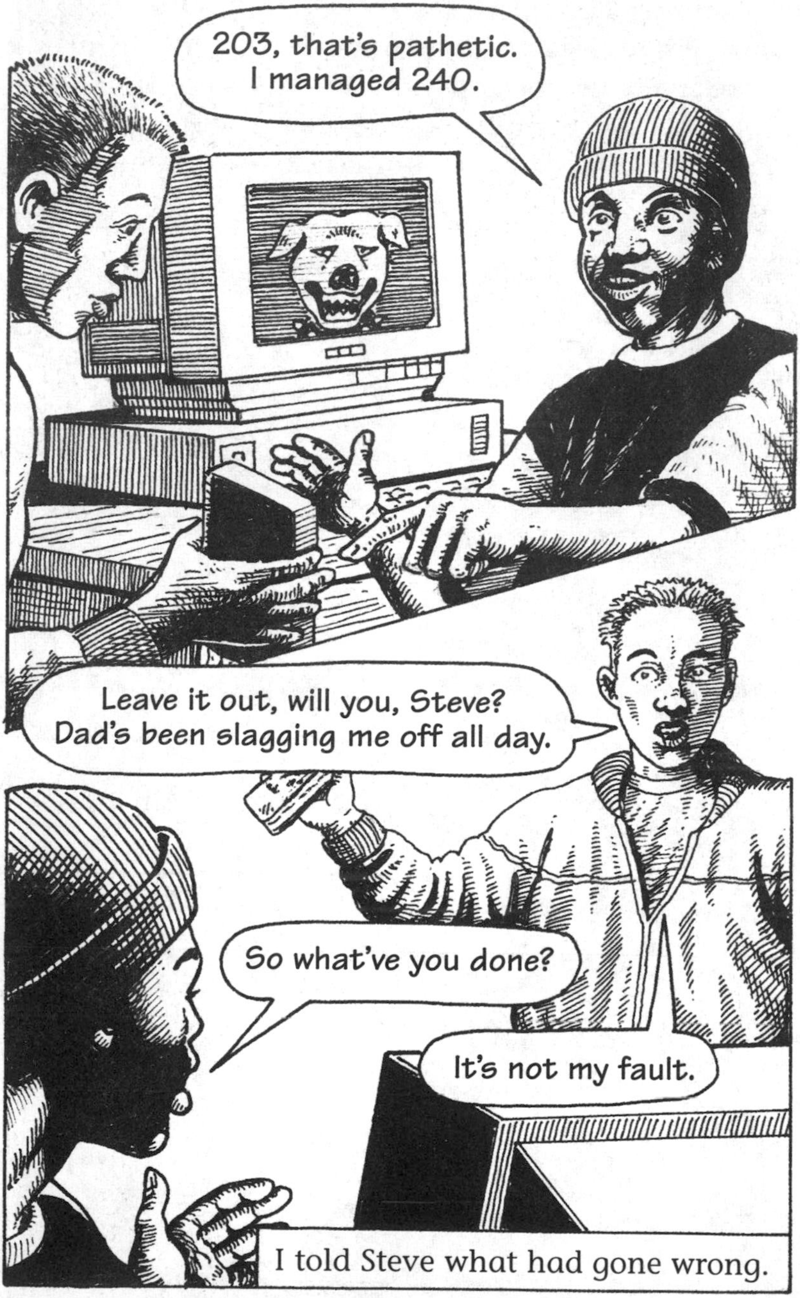
203, that's pathetic.
I managed 240.
Leave it out, will you, Steve?
Dad's been slagging me off all day.
So what've you done?
It's not my fault.

I told Steve what had gone wrong.

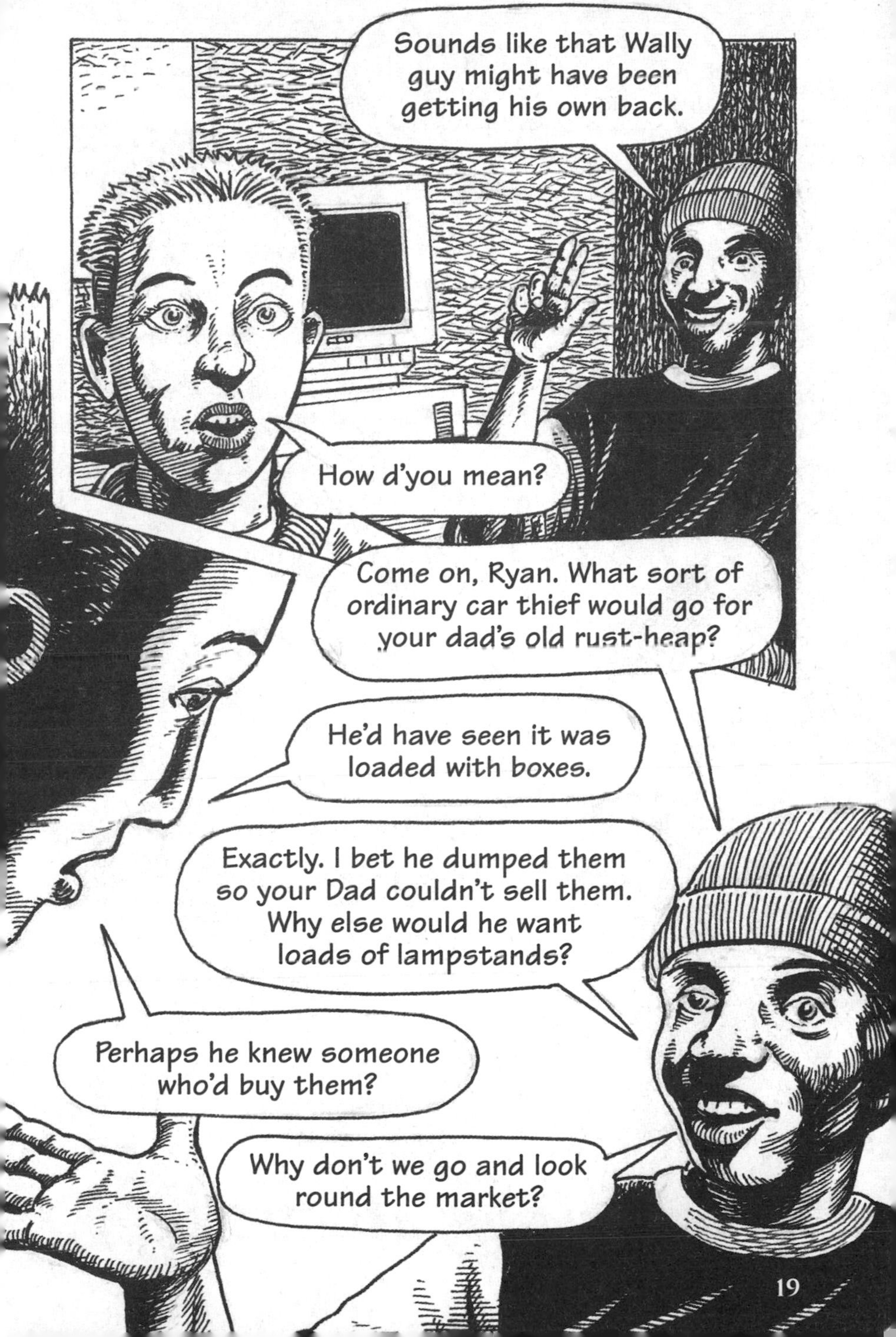
Sounds like that Wally guy might have been getting his own back.
How d'you mean?
Come on, Ryan. What sort of ordinary car thief would go for your dad's old rust-heap?
He'd have seen it was loaded with boxes.
Exactly. I bet he dumped them so your Dad couldn't sell them. Why else would he want loads of lampstands?
Perhaps he knew someone who'd buy them?
Why don't we go and look round the market?

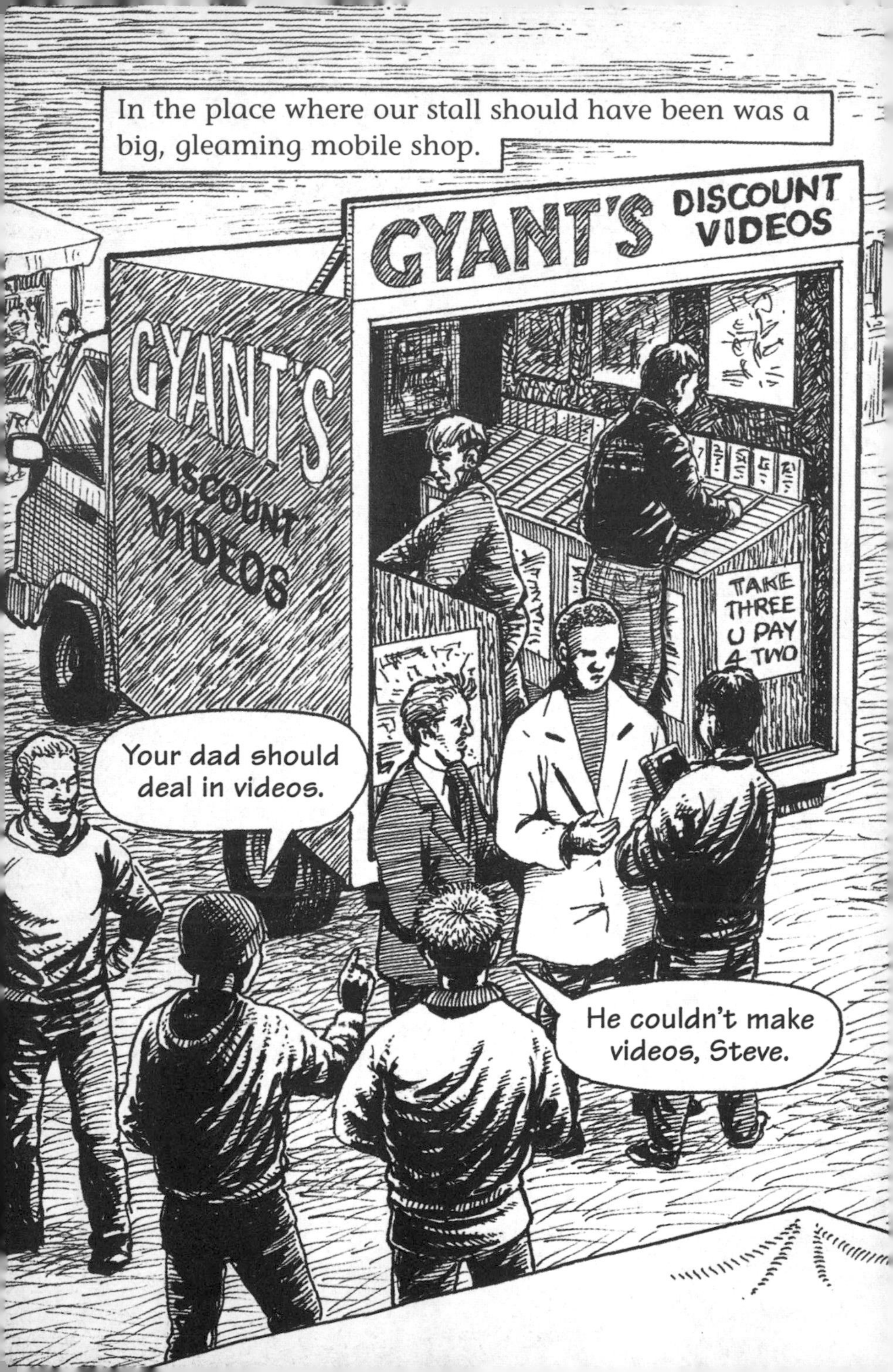
In the place where our stall should have been was a big, gleaming mobile shop.
GYANT'S DISCOUNT VIDEOS
GYANT'S DISCOUNT VIDEOS
TAKE THREE U PAY 4 TWO
Your dad should deal in videos.
He couldn't make videos, Steve.

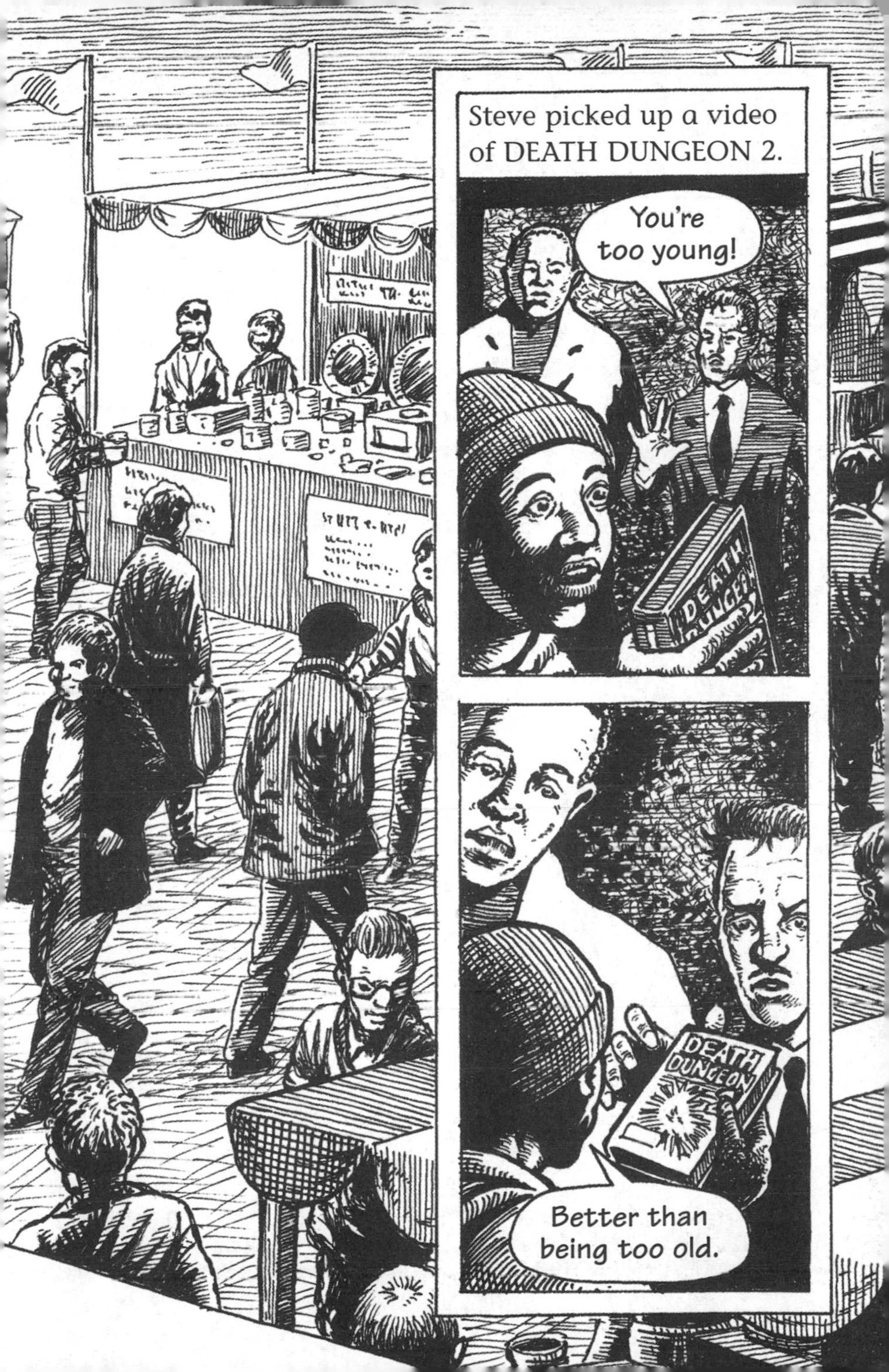

Steve picked up a video of DEATH DUNGEON 2.
You're too young!
DEATH DUNGEON
DEATH DUNGEON
Better than being too old.

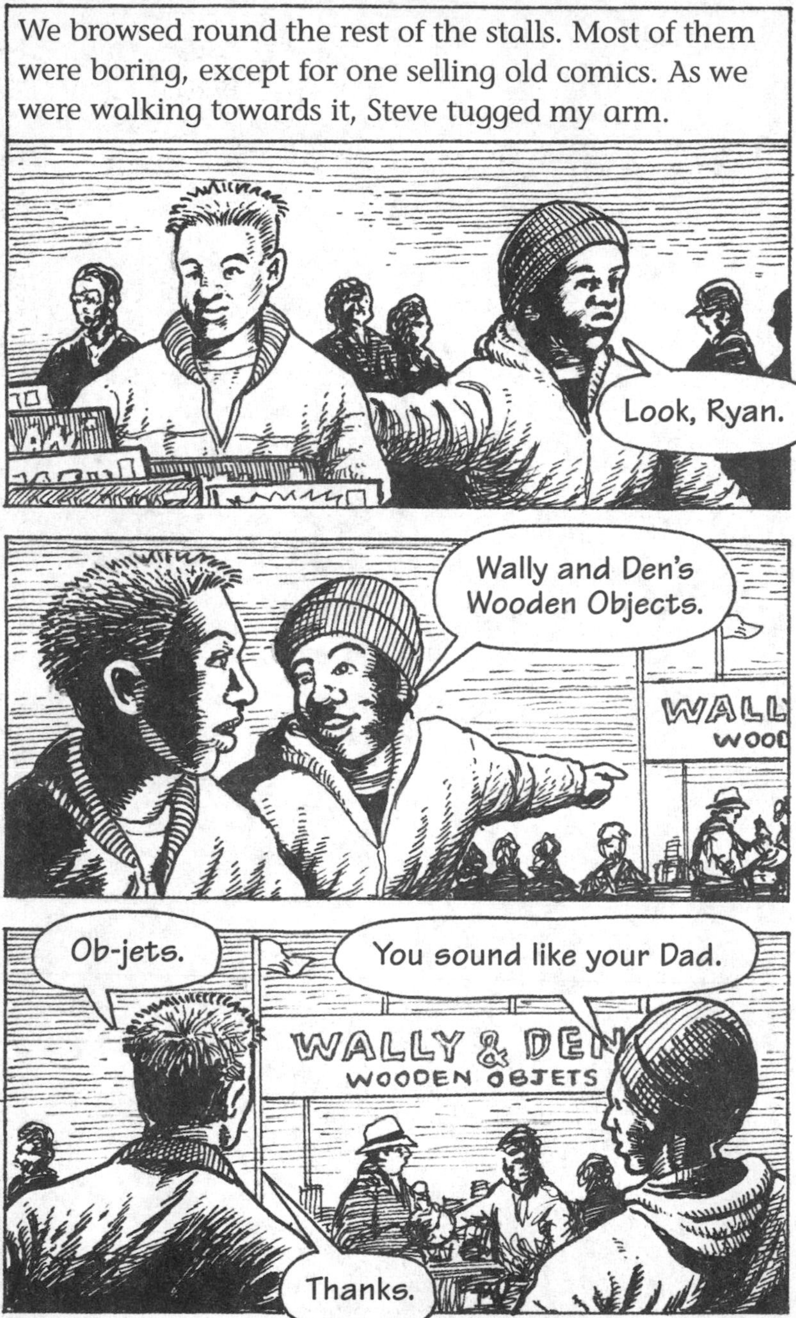
We browsed round the rest of the stalls. Most of them were boring, except for one selling old comics. As we were walking towards it, Steve tugged my arm.
Look, Ryan.
Wally and Den's Wooden Objects.
Ob-jets.
You sound like your Dad.
WALLY &
WOODEN OBJETS
Thanks.

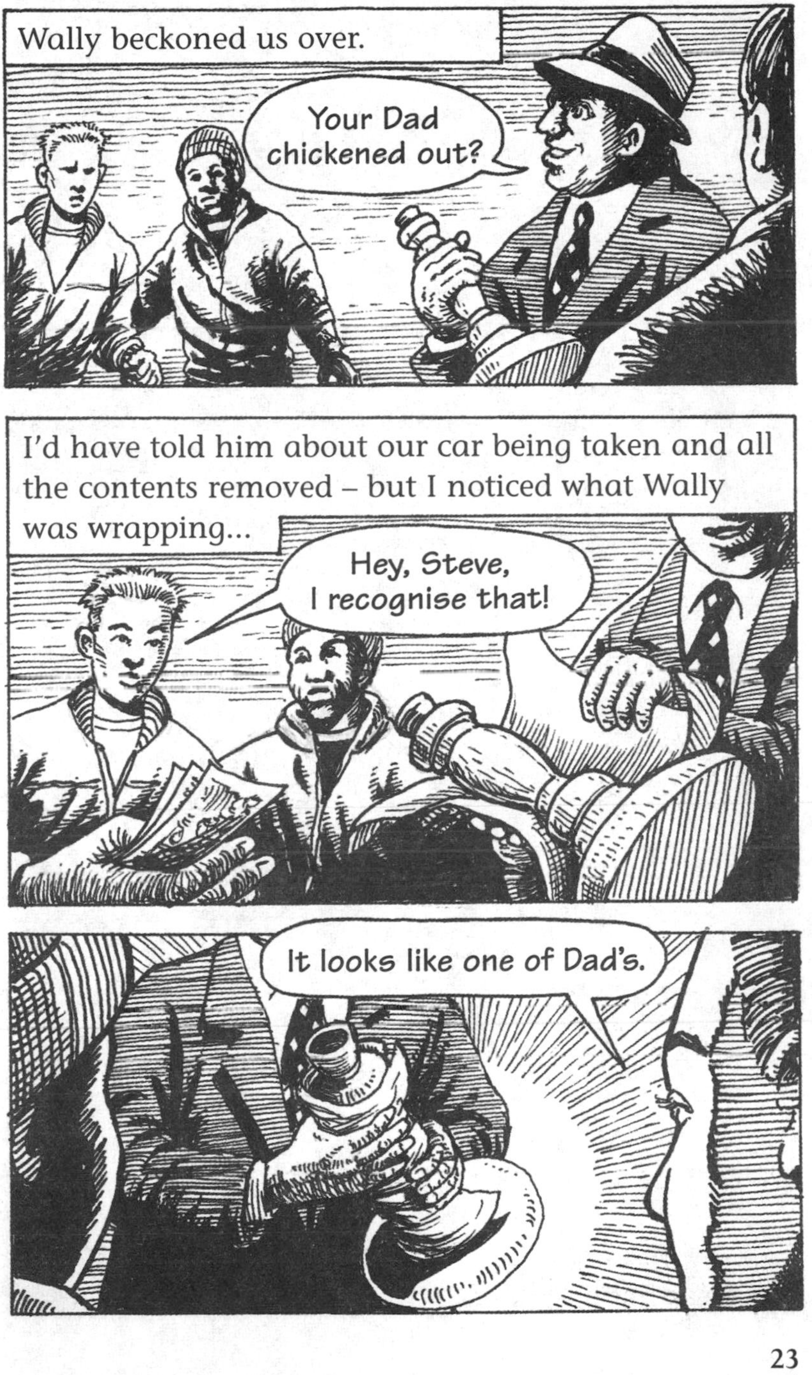
Wally beckoned us over.
Your Dad chickened out?
I'd have told him about our car being taken and all the contents removed – but I noticed what Wally was wrapping...
Hey, Steve, I recognise that!
It looks like one of Dad's.

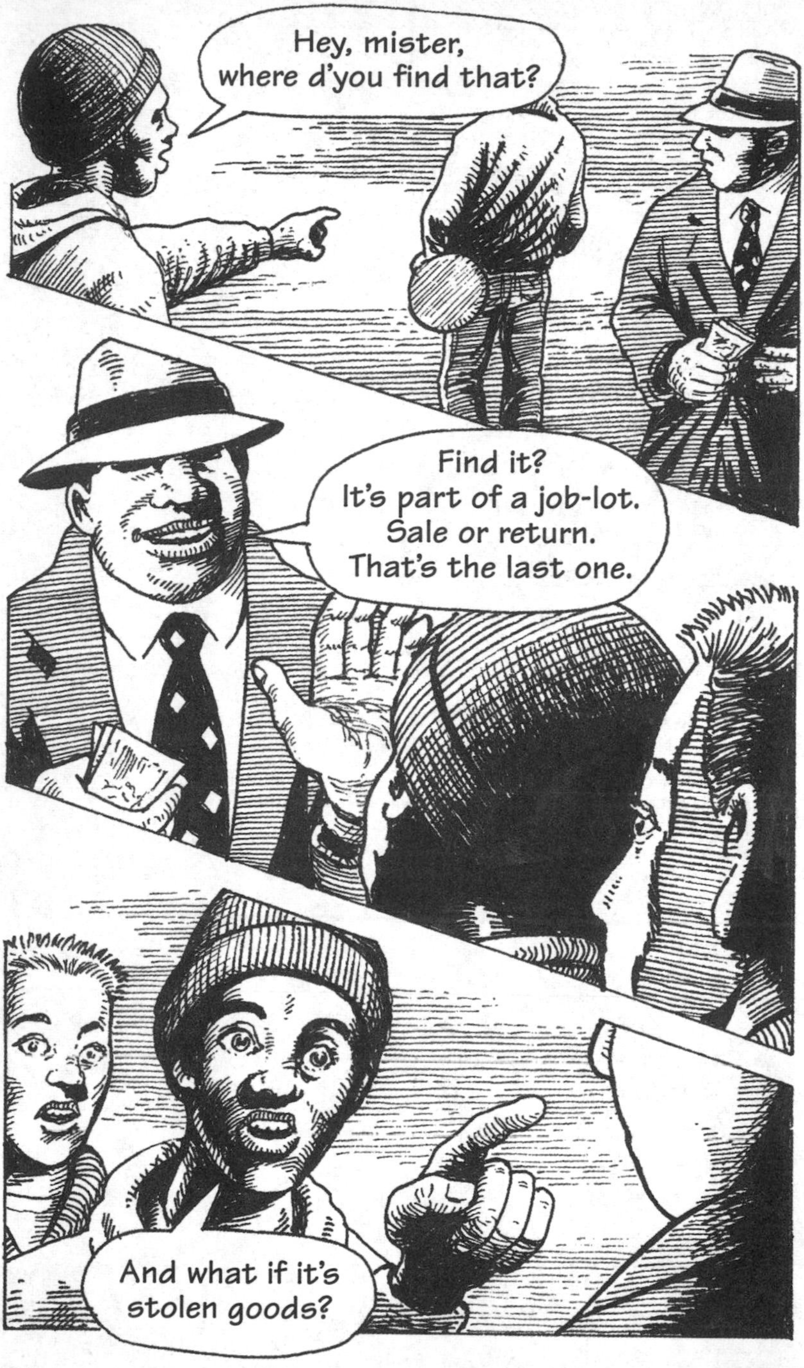
Hey, mister,
where d'you find that?
Find it?
It's part of a job-lot.
Sale or return.
That's the last one.
And what if it's
stolen goods?

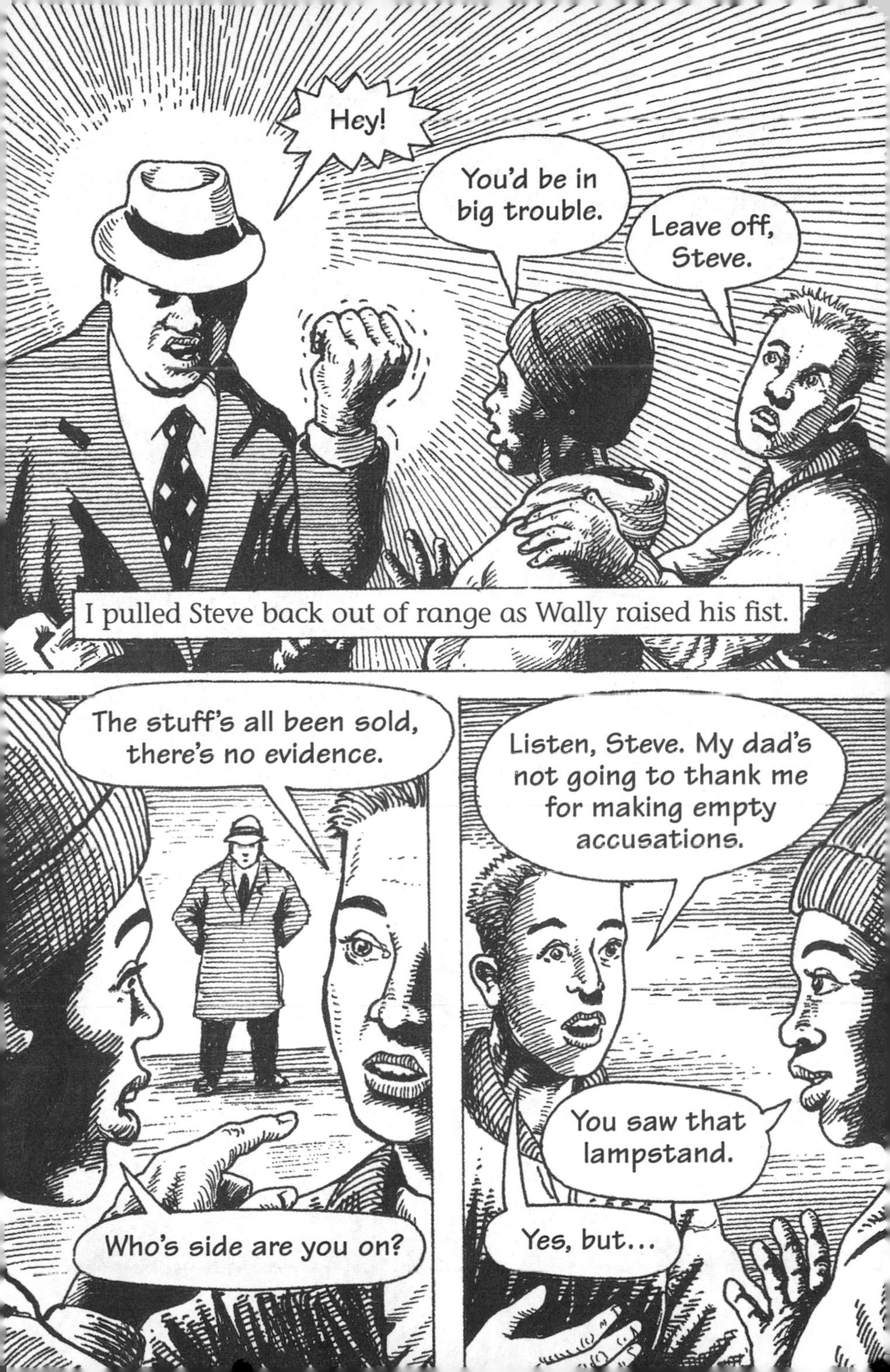
Hey!
You'd be in big trouble.
Leave off, Steve.
I pulled Steve back out of range as Wally raised his fist.
The stuff's all been sold, there's no evidence.
Who's side are you on?
Listen, Steve. My dad's not going to thank me for making empty accusations.
You saw that lampstand.
Yes, but...

I looked back at Wally's stall. Somebody else was there now, a man in a black leather jacket. Wally slipped him a fat brown envelope, and as the man walked away, I saw the back of his jacket.

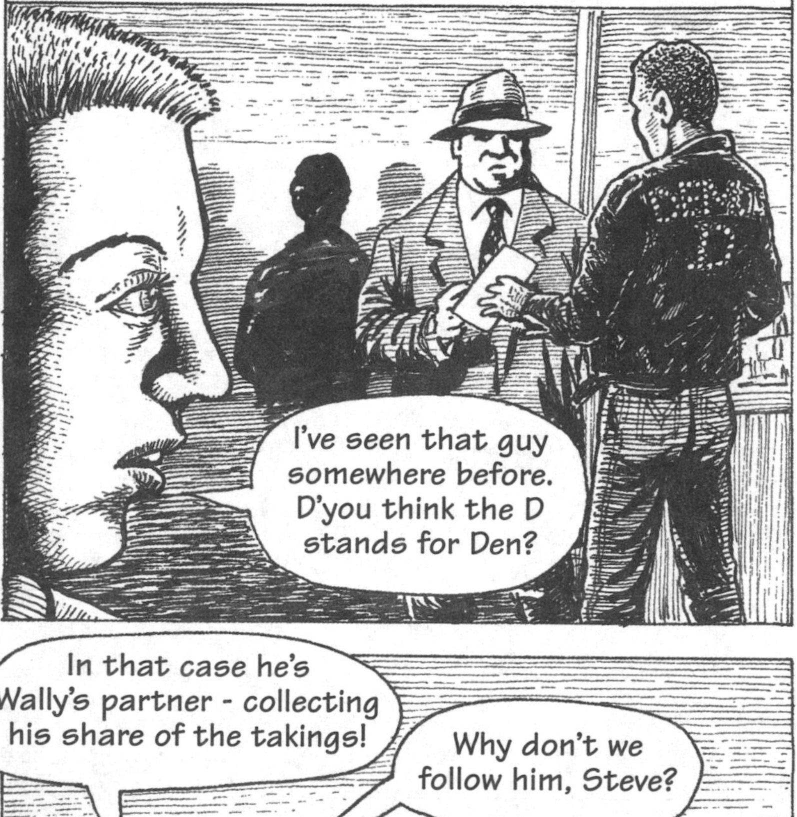
I've seen that guy somewhere before. D'you think the D stands for Den?

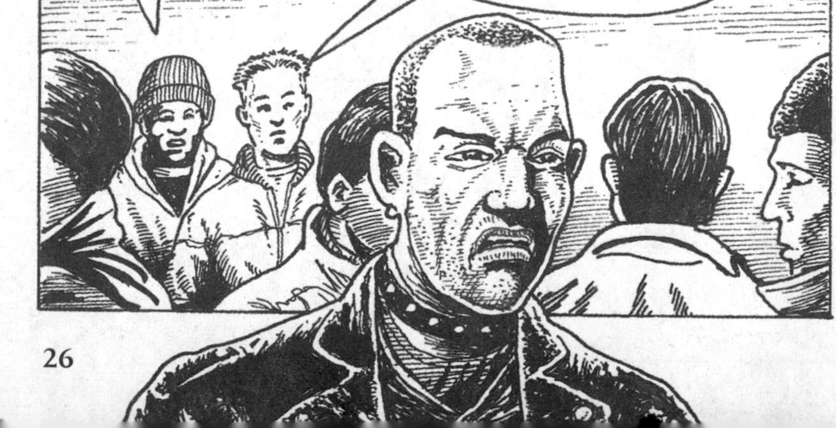
In that case he's Wally's partner - collecting his share of the takings!
Why don't we follow him, Steve?

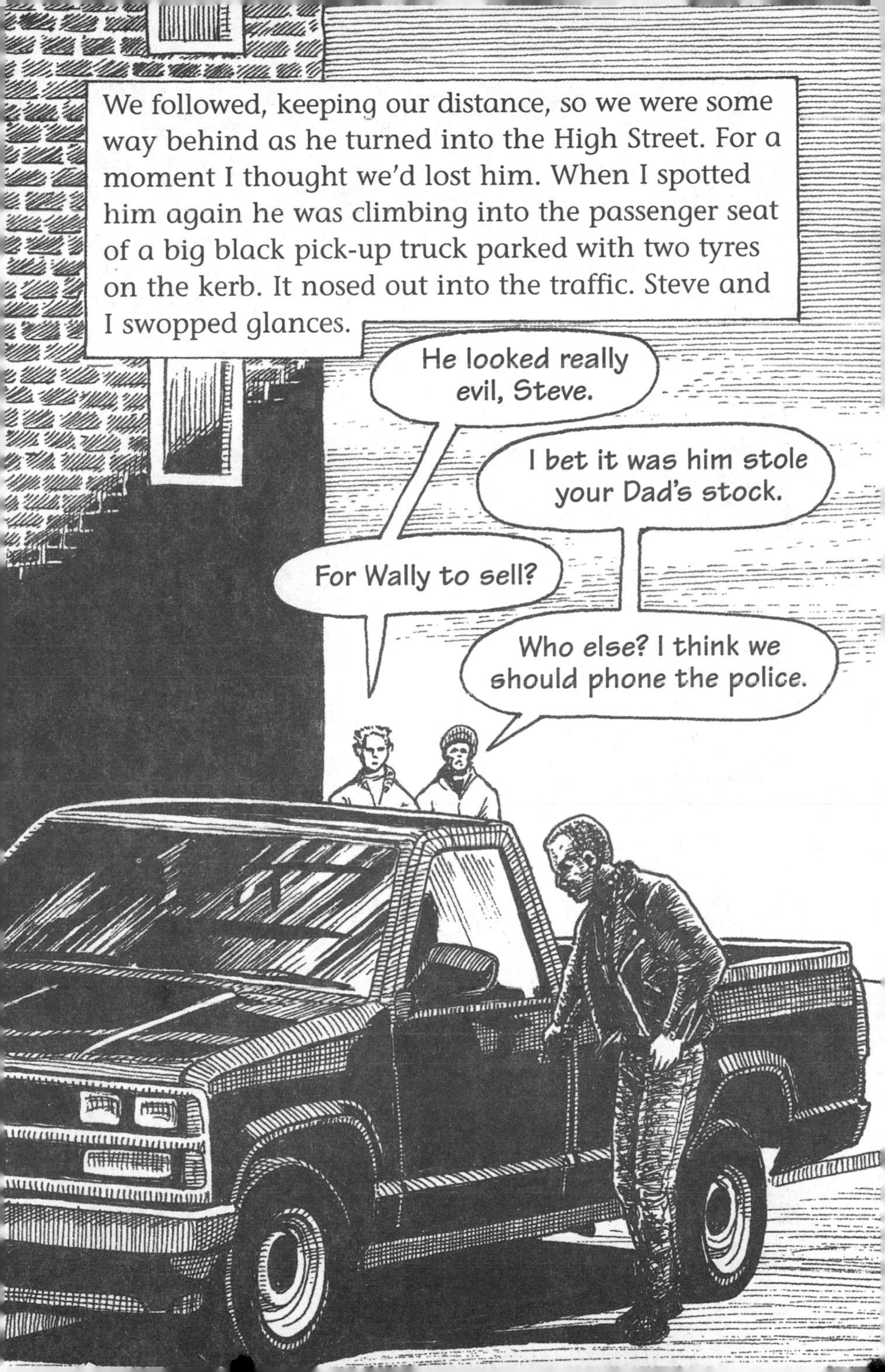
We followed, keeping our distance, so we were some way behind as he turned into the High Street. For a moment I thought we'd lost him. When I spotted him again he was climbing into the passenger seat of a big black pick-up truck parked with two tyres on the kerb. It nosed out into the traffic. Steve and I swopped glances.
He looked really evil, Steve.
I bet it was him stole your Dad's stock.
For Wally to sell?
Who else? I think we should phone the police.

Chapter Four

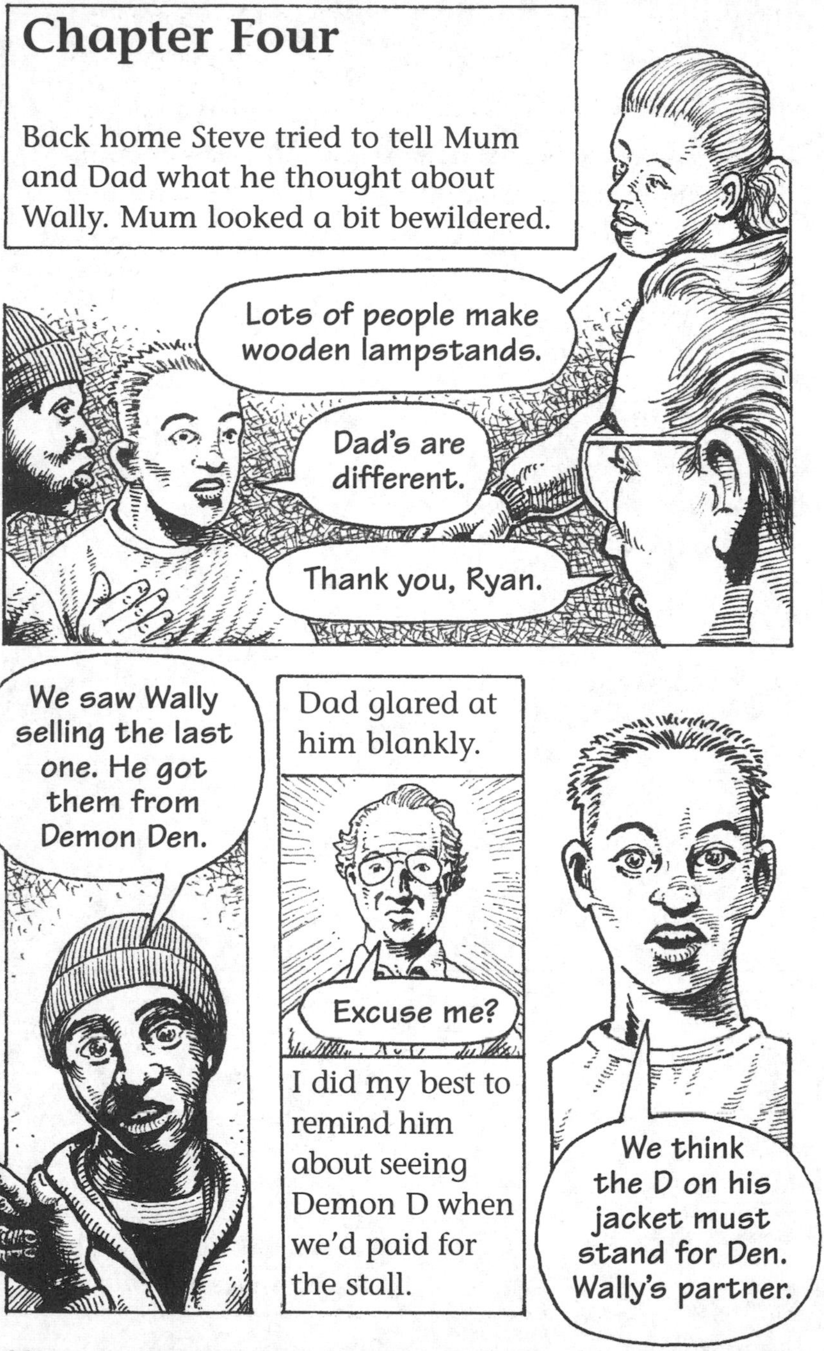
Back home Steve tried to tell Mum and Dad what he thought about Wally. Mum looked a bit bewildered.
Lots of people make wooden lampstands.
Dad's are different.
Thank you, Ryan.
We saw Wally selling the last one. He got them from Demon Den.
Dad glared at him blankly.
Excuse me?
I did my best to remind him about seeing Demon D when we'd paid for the stall.
We think the D on his jacket must stand for Den. Wally's partner.

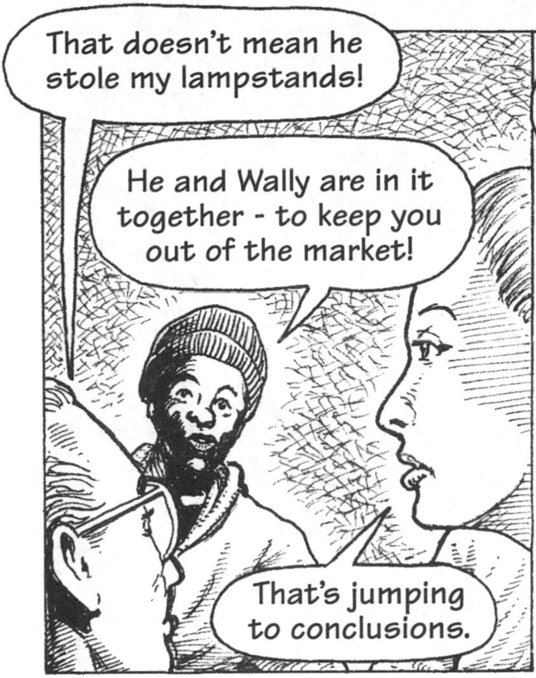
That doesn't mean he stole my lampstands!
He and Wally are in it together - to keep you out of the market!
That's jumping to conclusions.

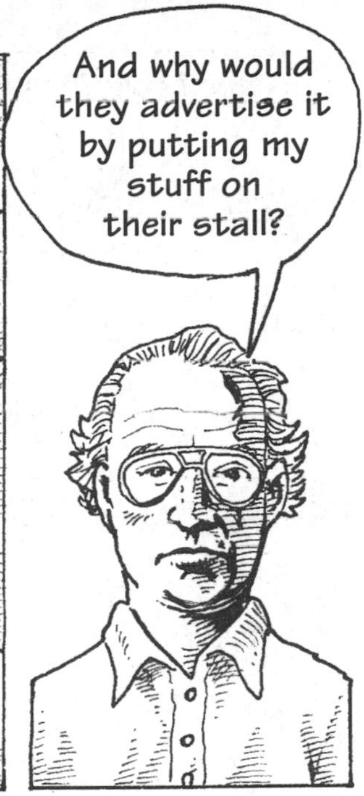
And why would they advertise it by putting my stuff on their stall?

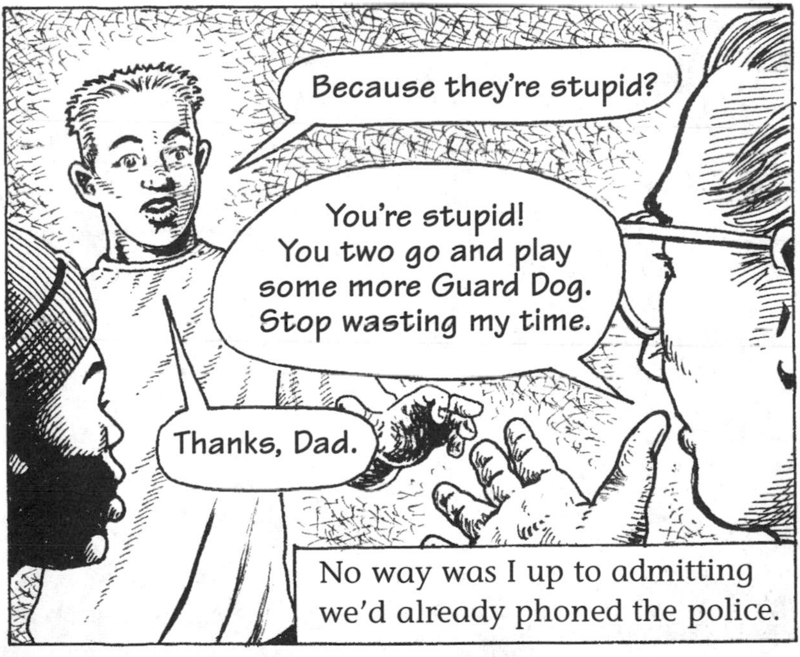
Because they're stupid?
You're stupid! You two go and play some more Guard Dog. Stop wasting my time.
Thanks, Dad.
No way was I up to admitting we'd already phoned the police.

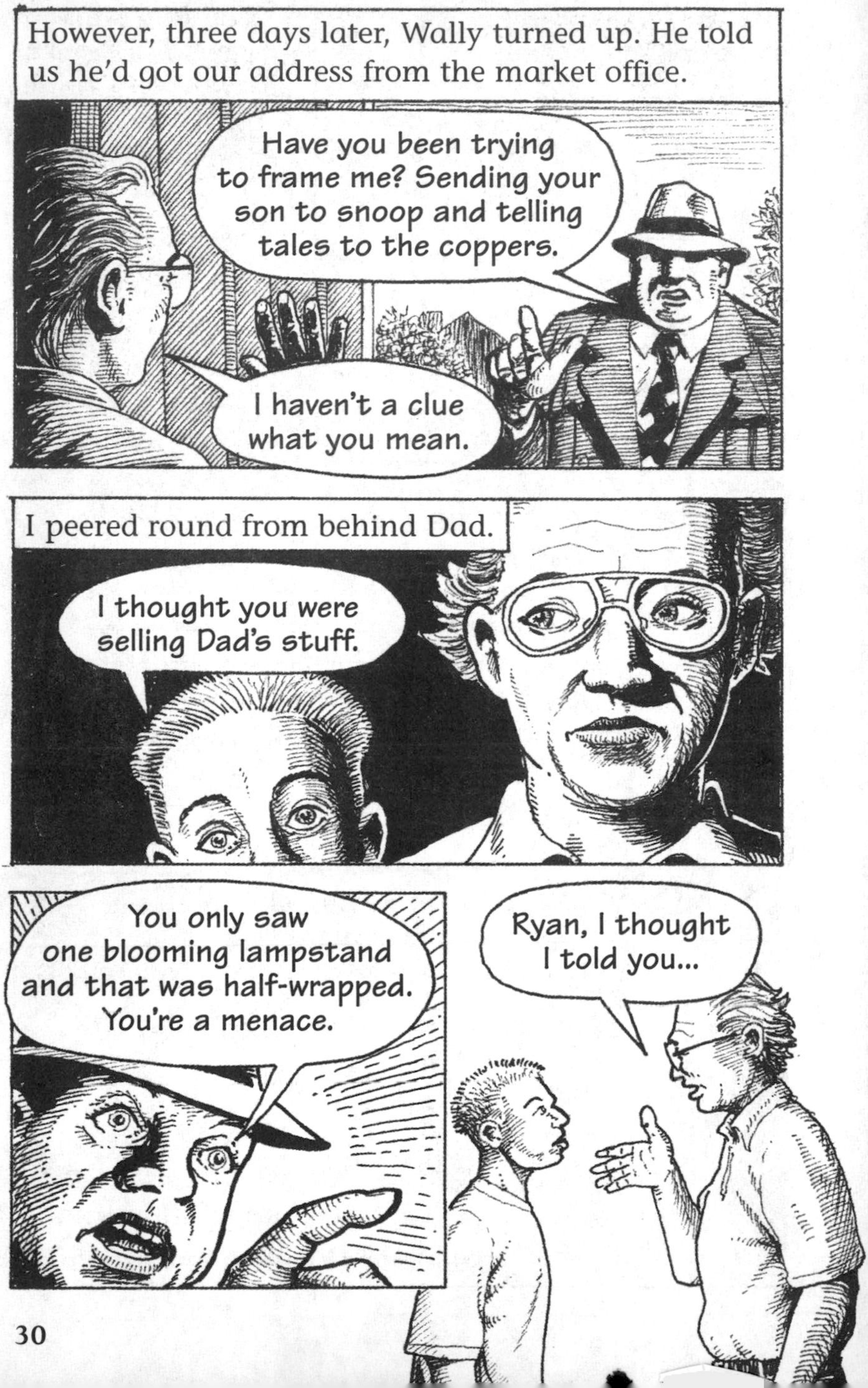
However, three days later, Wally turned up. He told us he'd got our address from the market office.
Have you been trying to frame me? Sending your son to snoop and telling tales to the coppers.
I haven't a clue what you mean.
I peered round from behind Dad.
I thought you were selling Dad's stuff.
You only saw one blooming lampstand and that was half-wrapped. You're a menace.
Ryan, I thought I told you...

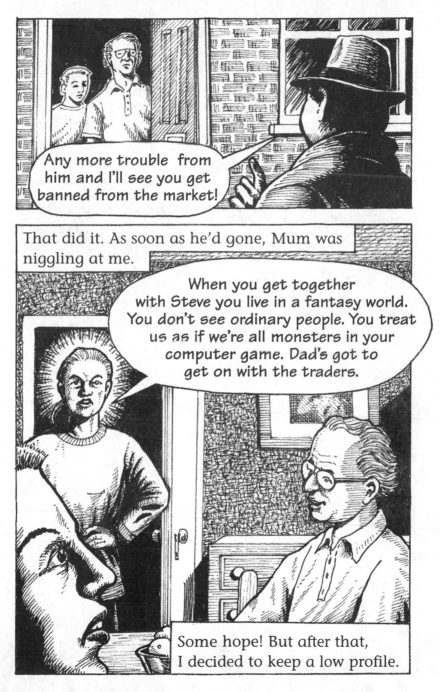

Any more trouble from him and I'll see you get banned from the market!

That did it. As soon as he'd gone, Mum was niggling at me.

When you get together with Steve you live in a fantasy world. You don't see ordinary people. You treat us as if we're all monsters in your computer game. Dad's got to get on with the traders.

Some hope! But after that, I decided to keep a low profile.

When I got home from school on Friday afternoon Dad was already busy lugging cardboard boxes out of his shed.

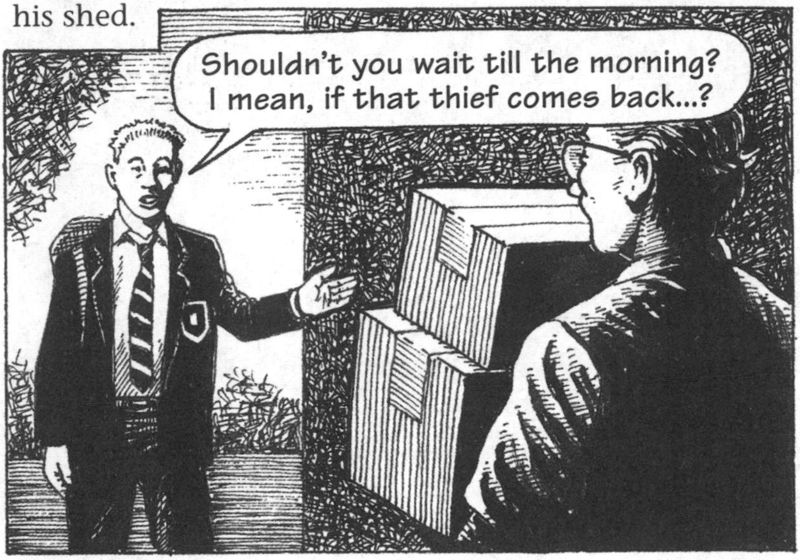
Shouldn't you wait till the morning? I mean, if that thief comes back...?

He gave me a clever look.

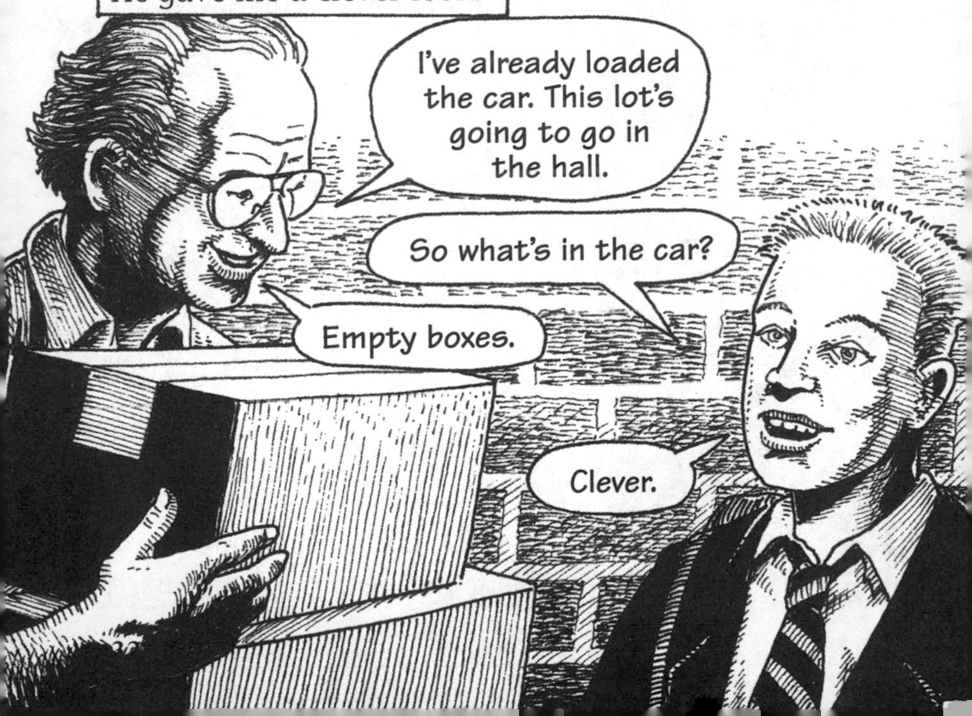
I've already loaded the car. This lot's going to go in the hall.
So what's in the car?
Empty boxes.
Clever.

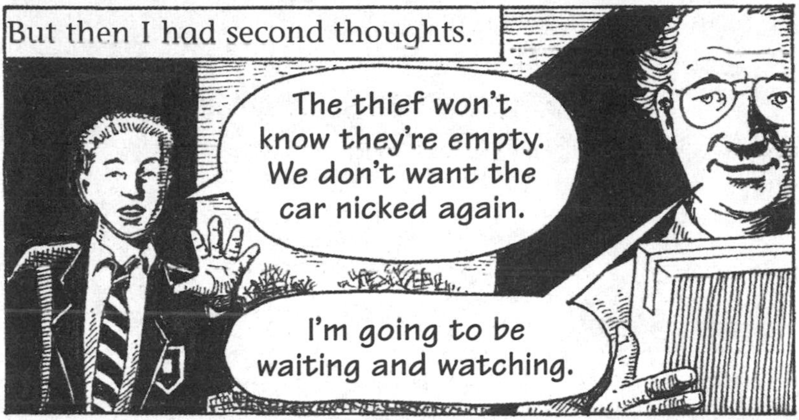
But then I had second thoughts.
The thief won't know they're empty. We don't want the car nicked again.
I'm going to be waiting and watching.

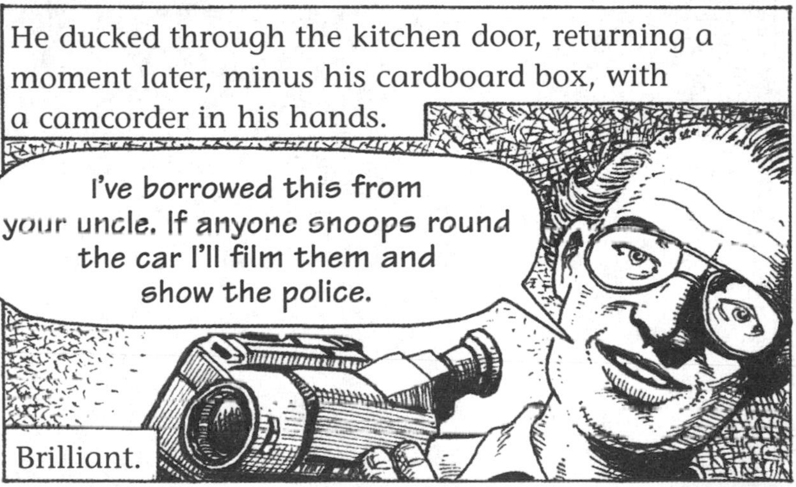
He ducked through the kitchen door, returning a moment later, minus his cardboard box, with a camcorder in his hands.
I've borrowed this from your uncle. If anyone snoops round the car I'll film them and show the police.
Brilliant.

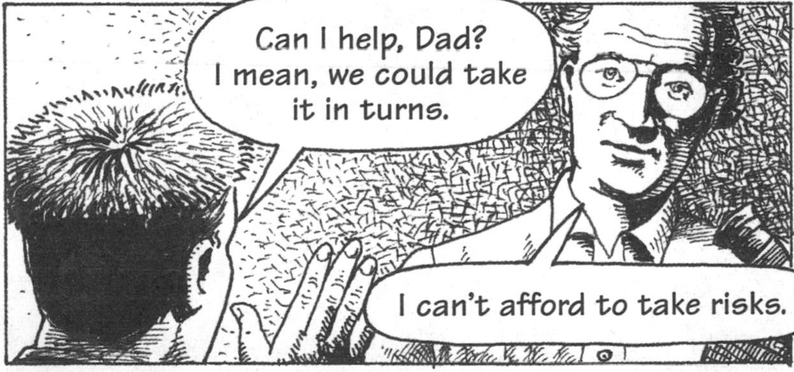
Can I help, Dad? I mean, we could take it in turns.
I can't afford to take risks.

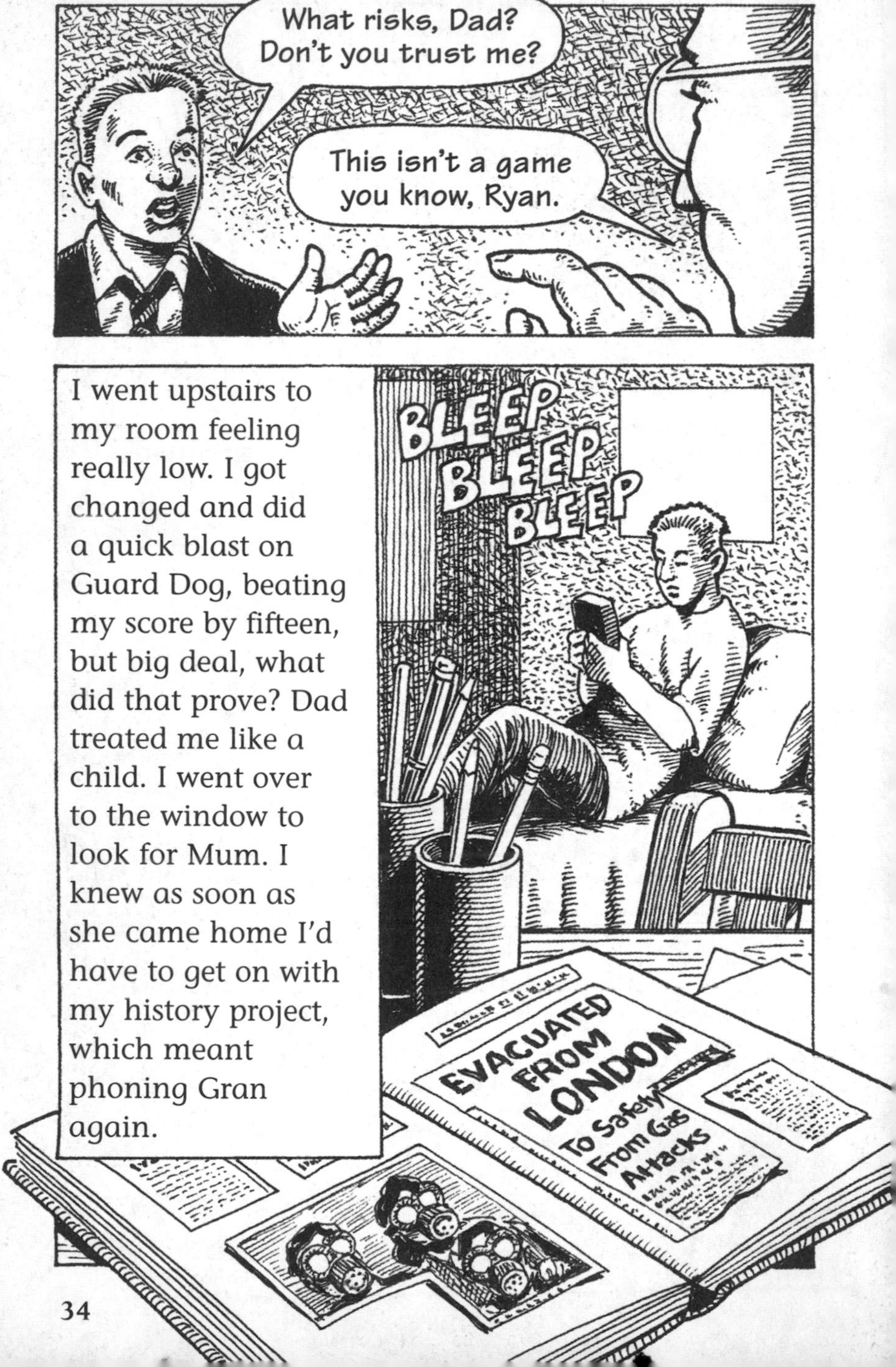
What risks, Dad? Don't you trust me?
This isn't a game you know, Ryan.
I went upstairs to my room feeling really low. I got changed and did a quick blast on Guard Dog, beating my score by fifteen, but big deal, what did that prove? Dad treated me like a child. I went over to the window to look for Mum. I knew as soon as she came home I'd have to get on with my history project, which meant phoning Gran again.
BLEEP BLEEP BLEEP
EVACUATED FROM LONDON
To Safety From Gas Attacks

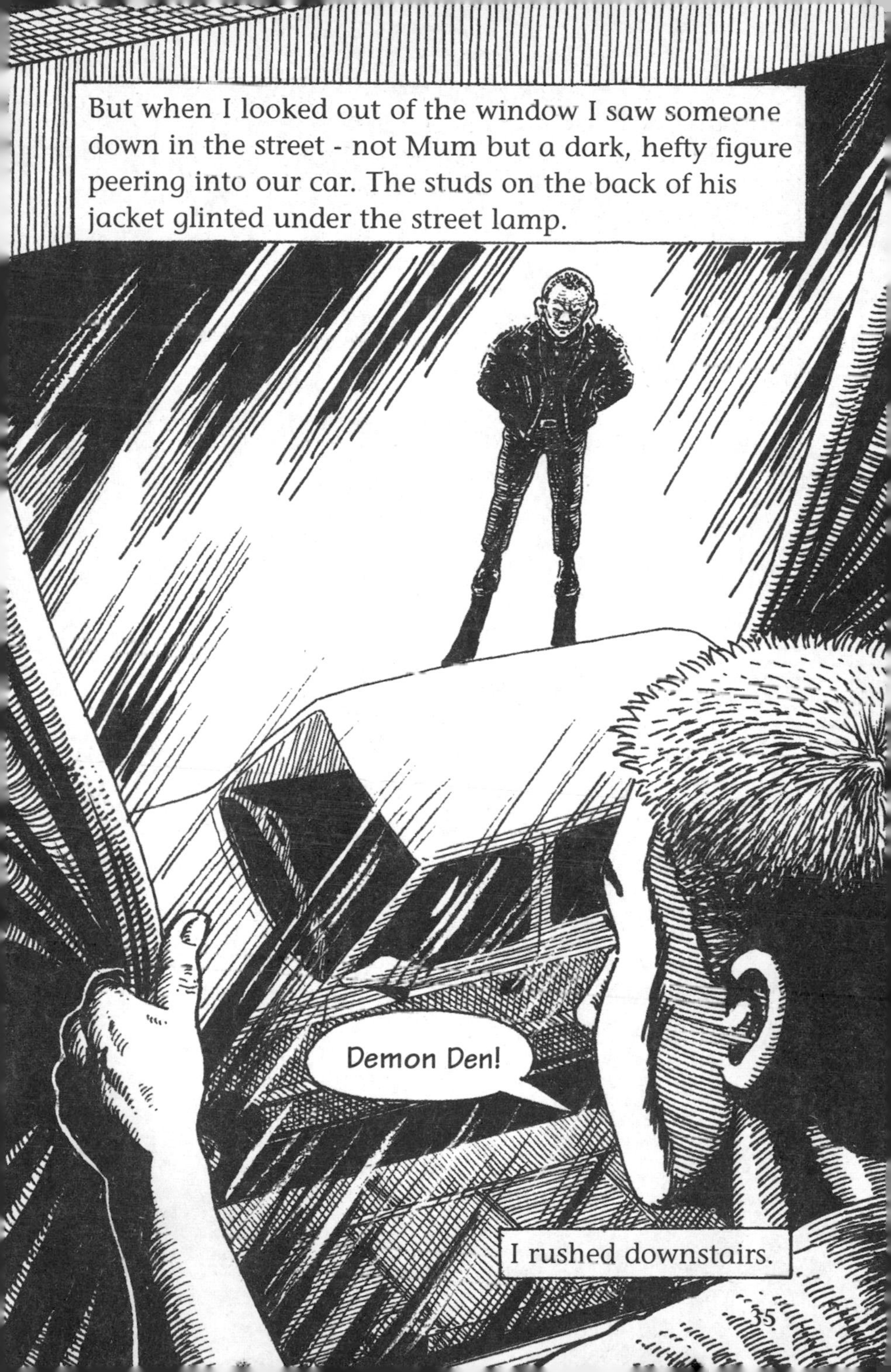
But when I looked out of the window I saw someone down in the street - not Mum but a dark, hefty figure peering into our car. The studs on the back of his jacket glinted under the street lamp.
Demon Den!
I rushed downstairs.

Chapter Five

I would have told Dad about Demon, but Dad had gone back to his shed, leaving the camcorder on the kitchen table. I picked it up.

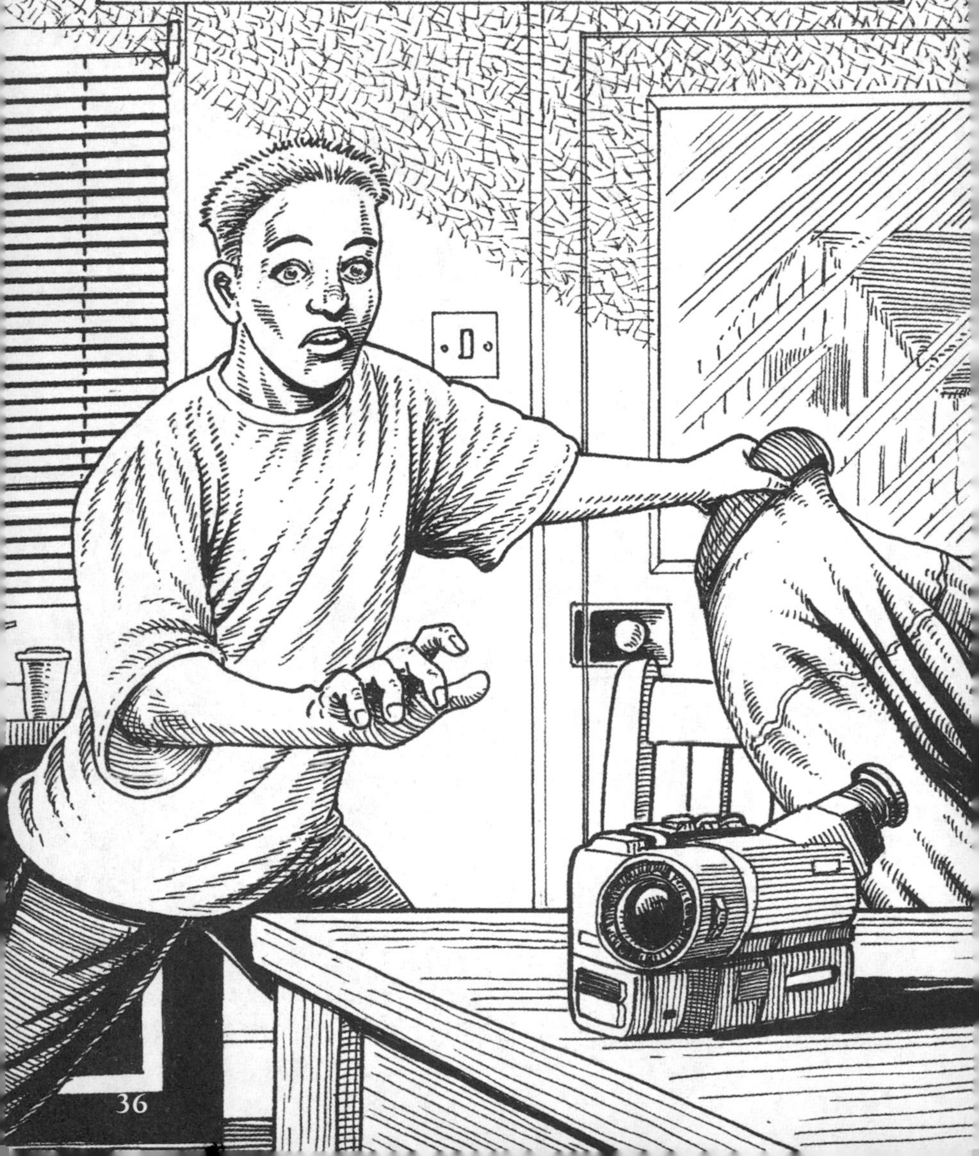

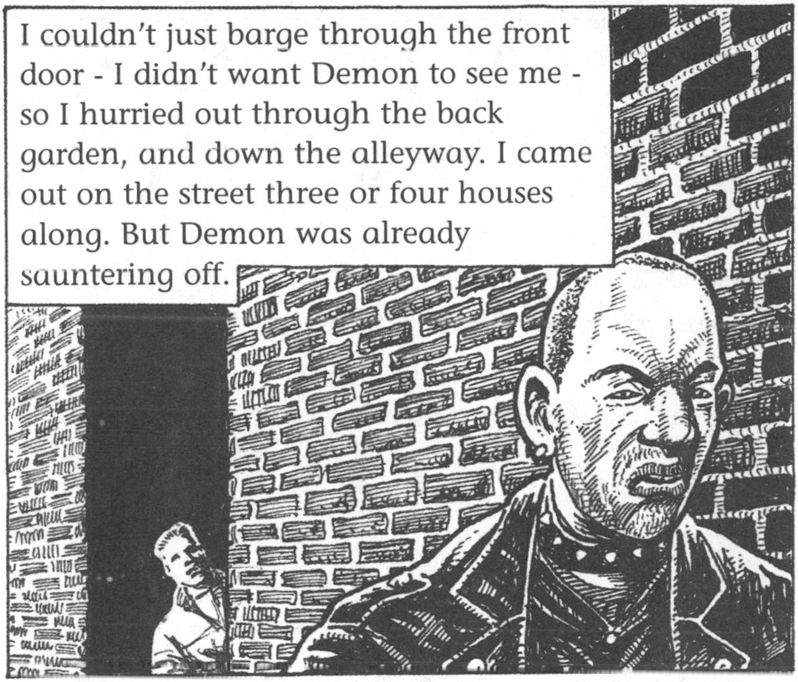
I couldn't just barge through the front door - I didn't want Demon to see me - so I hurried out through the back garden, and down the alleyway. I came out on the street three or four houses along. But Demon was already sauntering off.

I trailed him to the station where he went into a phone booth next to the taxi rank. I waited, wanting to film him, but there was no light in the booth. No matter, I heard him all right, spitting words into the phone.

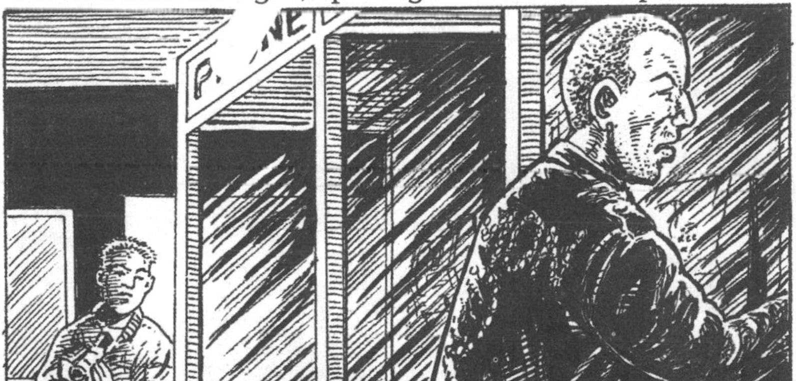

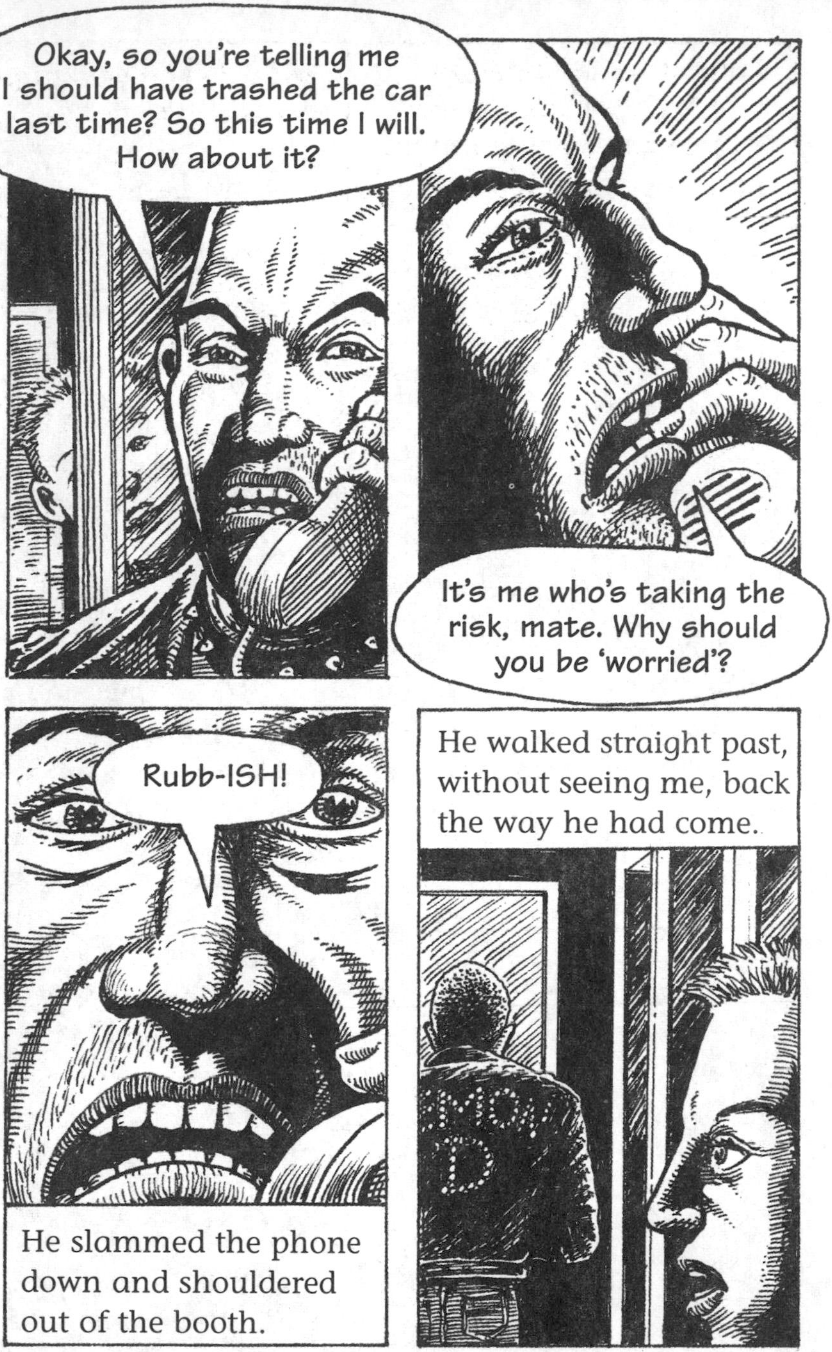
Okay, so you're telling me I should have trashed the car last time? So this time I will. How about it?
It's me who's taking the risk, mate. Why should you be 'worried'?
Rubb-ISH!
He slammed the phone down and shouldered out of the booth.
He walked straight past, without seeing me, back the way he had come.

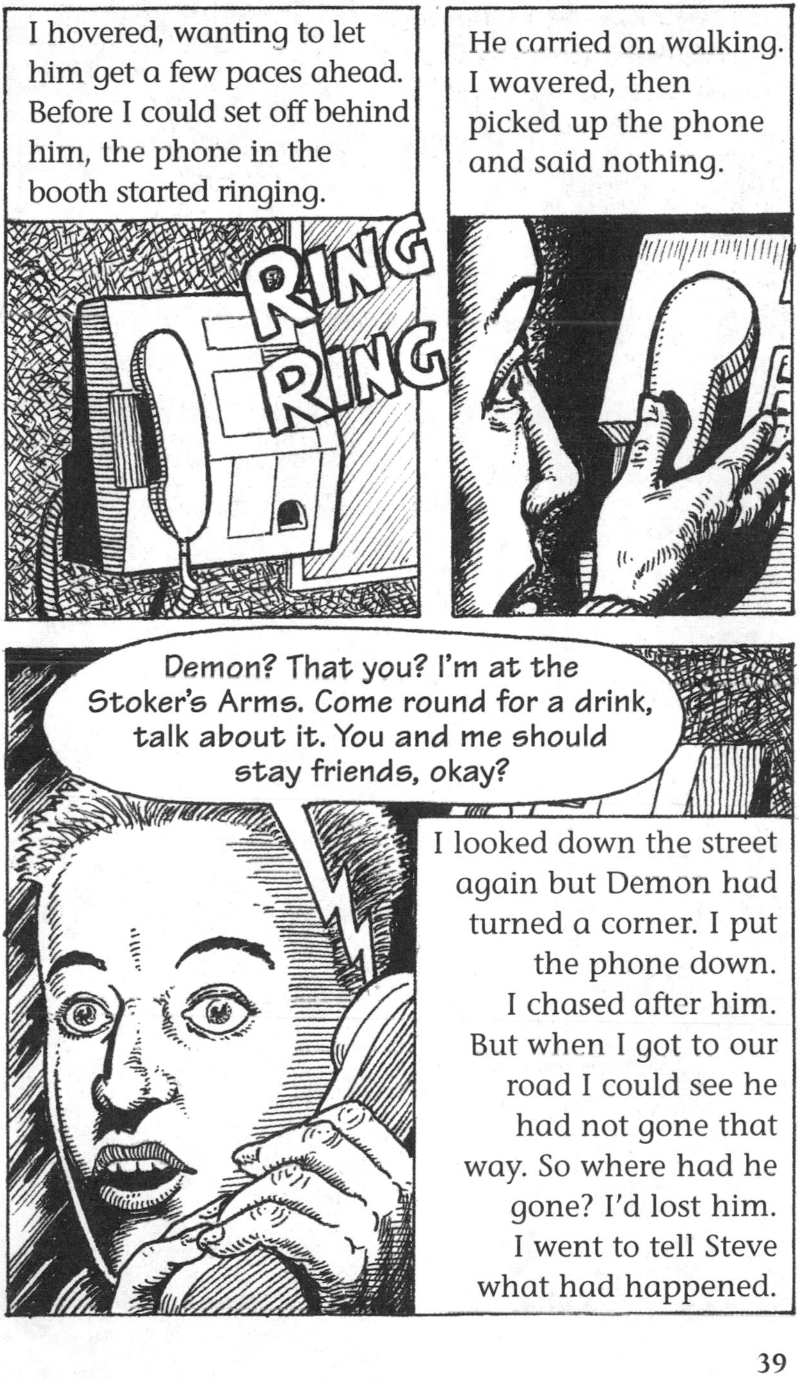
I hovered, wanting to let him get a few paces ahead. Before I could set off behind him, the phone in the booth started ringing.
RING RING
He carried on walking. I wavered, then picked up the phone and said nothing.
Demon? That you? I'm at the Stoker's Arms. Come round for a drink, talk about it. You and me should stay friends, okay?
I looked down the street again but Demon had turned a corner. I put the phone down. I chased after him. But when I got to our road I could see he had not gone that way. So where had he gone? I'd lost him. I went to tell Steve what had happened.

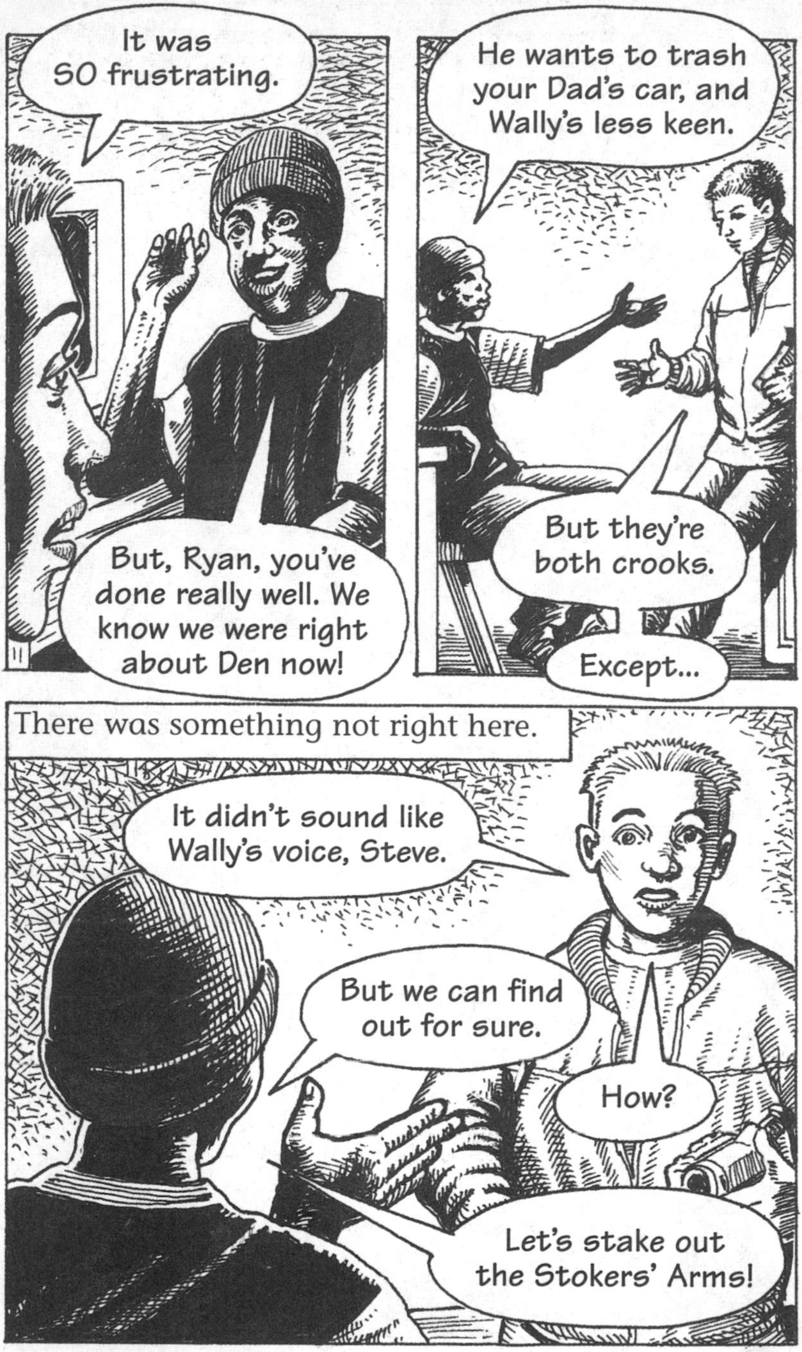
It was SO frustrating.
But, Ryan, you've done really well. We know we were right about Den now!
He wants to trash your Dad's car, and Wally's less keen.
But they're both crooks.
Except...
There was something not right here.
It didn't sound like Wally's voice, Steve.
But we can find out for sure.
How?
Let's stake out the Stokers' Arms!

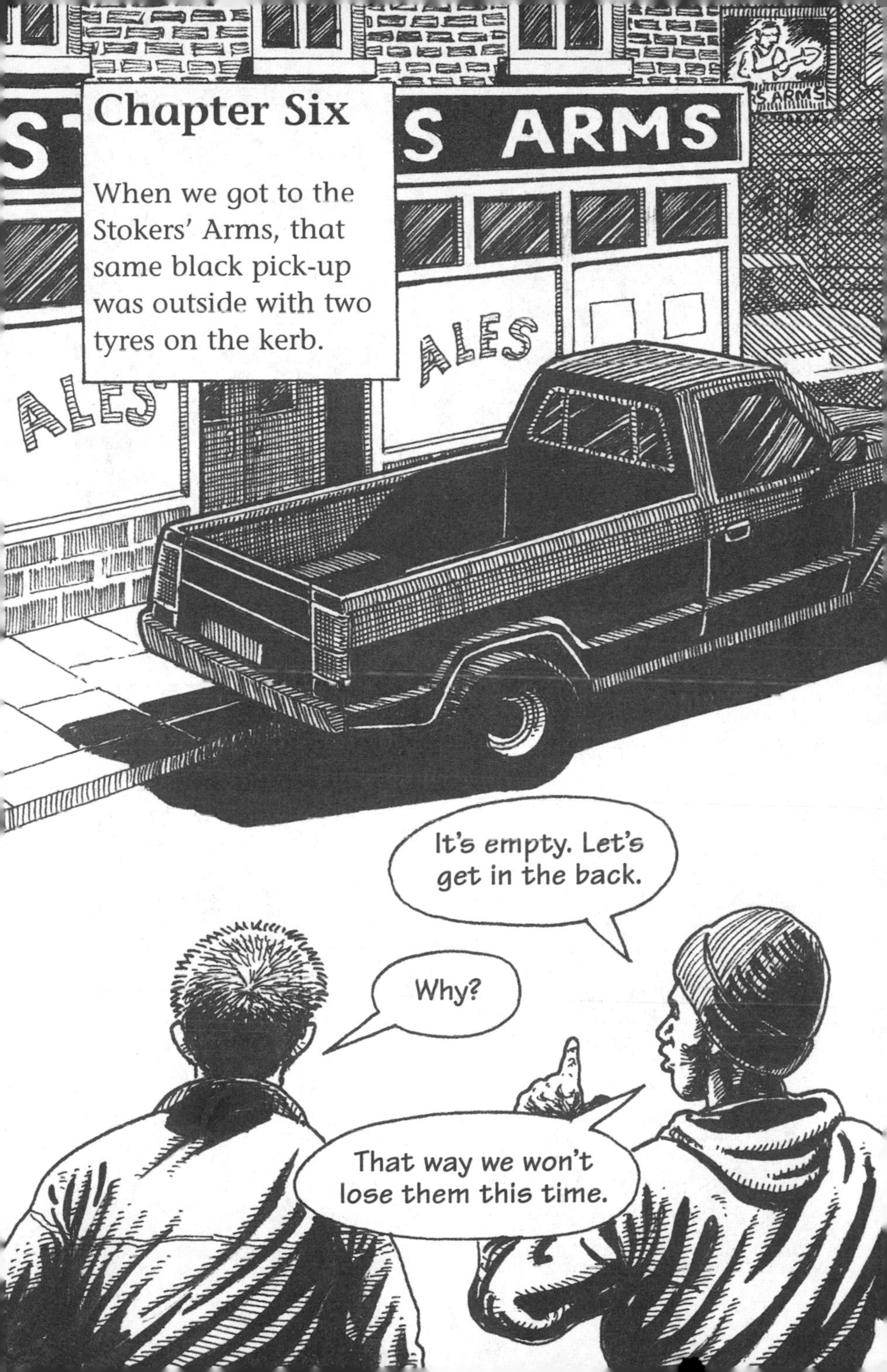
Chapter Six
When we got to the Stokers' Arms, that same black pick-up was outside with two tyres on the kerb.
S ARMS
ALES
ALES
It's empty. Let's get in the back.
Why?
That way we won't lose them this time.

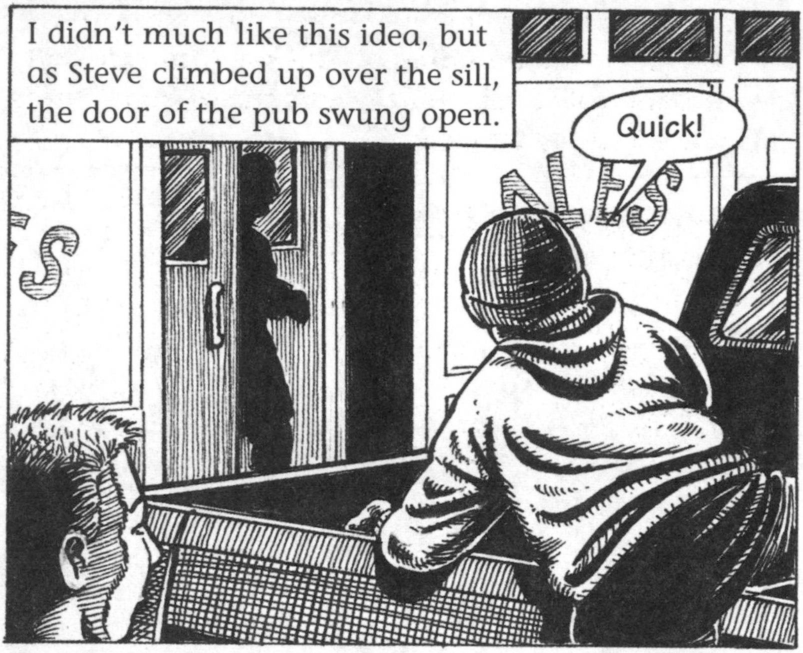
I didn't much like this idea, but as Steve climbed up over the sill, the door of the pub swung open.
Quick!

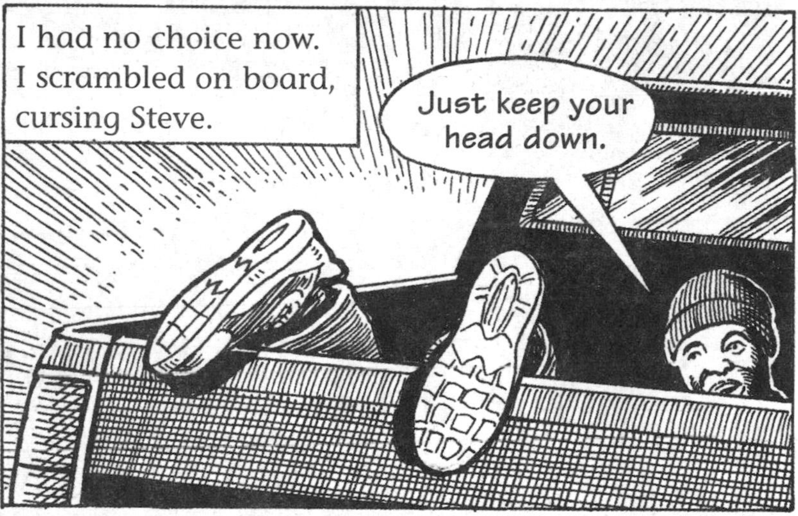
I had no choice now. I scrambled on board, cursing Steve.
Just keep your head down.

We ducked out of sight. Someone climbed into the pick-up's cab, and started the engine.

A door slammed, the engine roared. The pick-up went lurching forward, bumping off the kerb, and we got shaken and rolled all over the cold metal floor. It was lucky the journey was short.

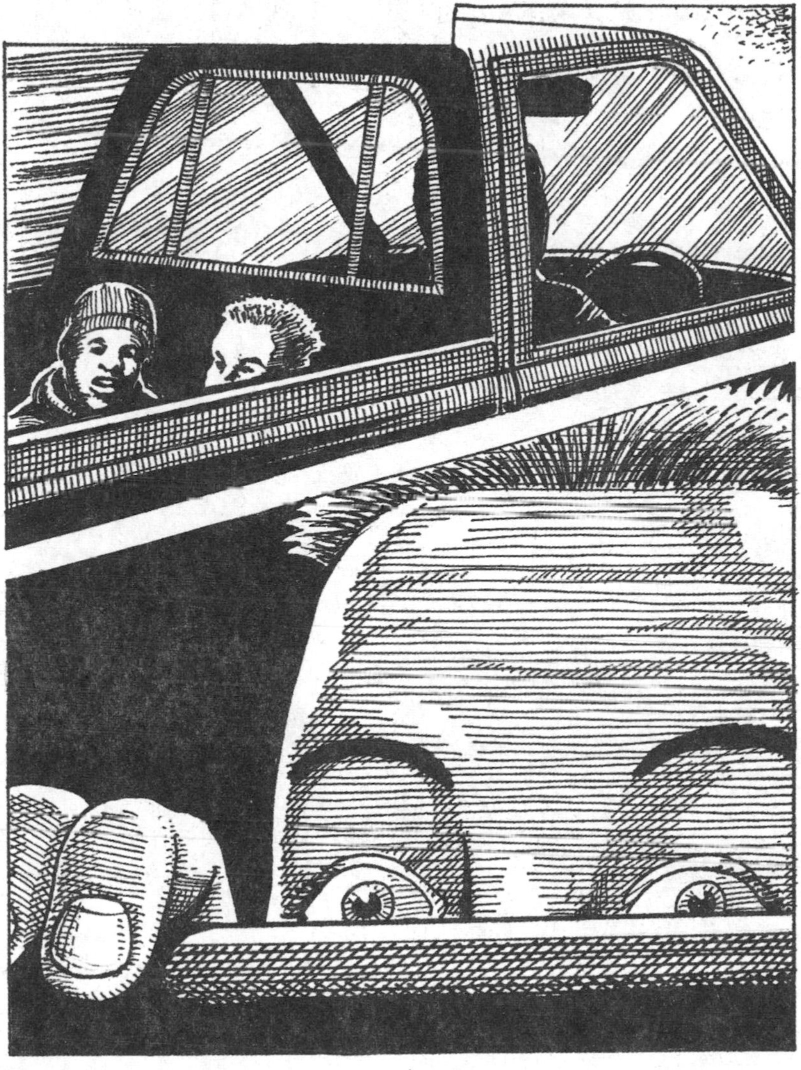

The truck veered down a dark back street and came to a stop. The man jumped out. I risked a look over the side.

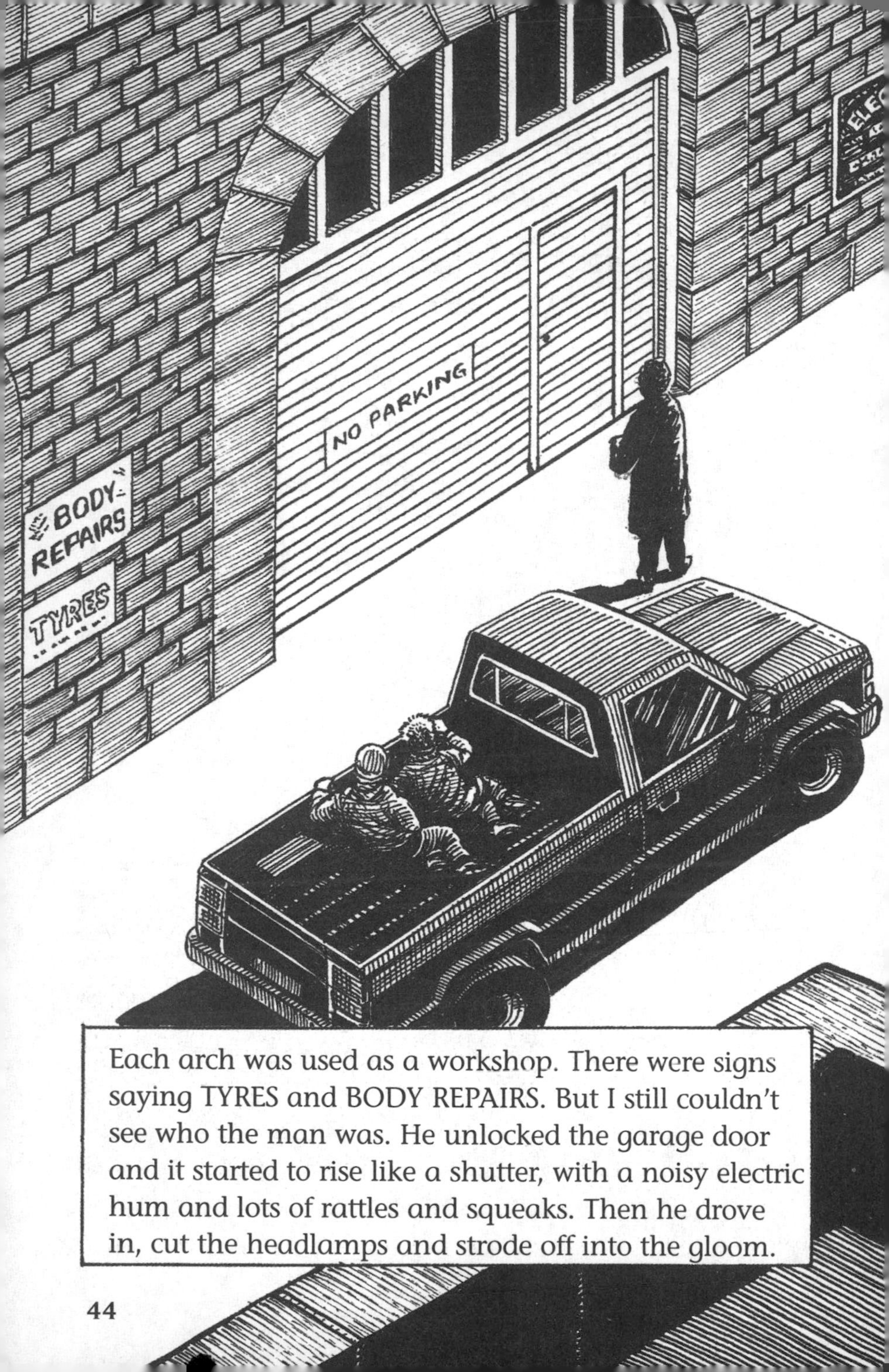
NO PARKING
BODY REPAIRS
TYRES

Each arch was used as a workshop. There were signs saying TYRES and BODY REPAIRS. But I still couldn't see who the man was. He unlocked the garage door and it started to rise like a shutter, with a noisy electric hum and lots of rattles and squeaks. Then he drove in, cut the headlamps and strode off into the gloom.

A door slammed down the far end.

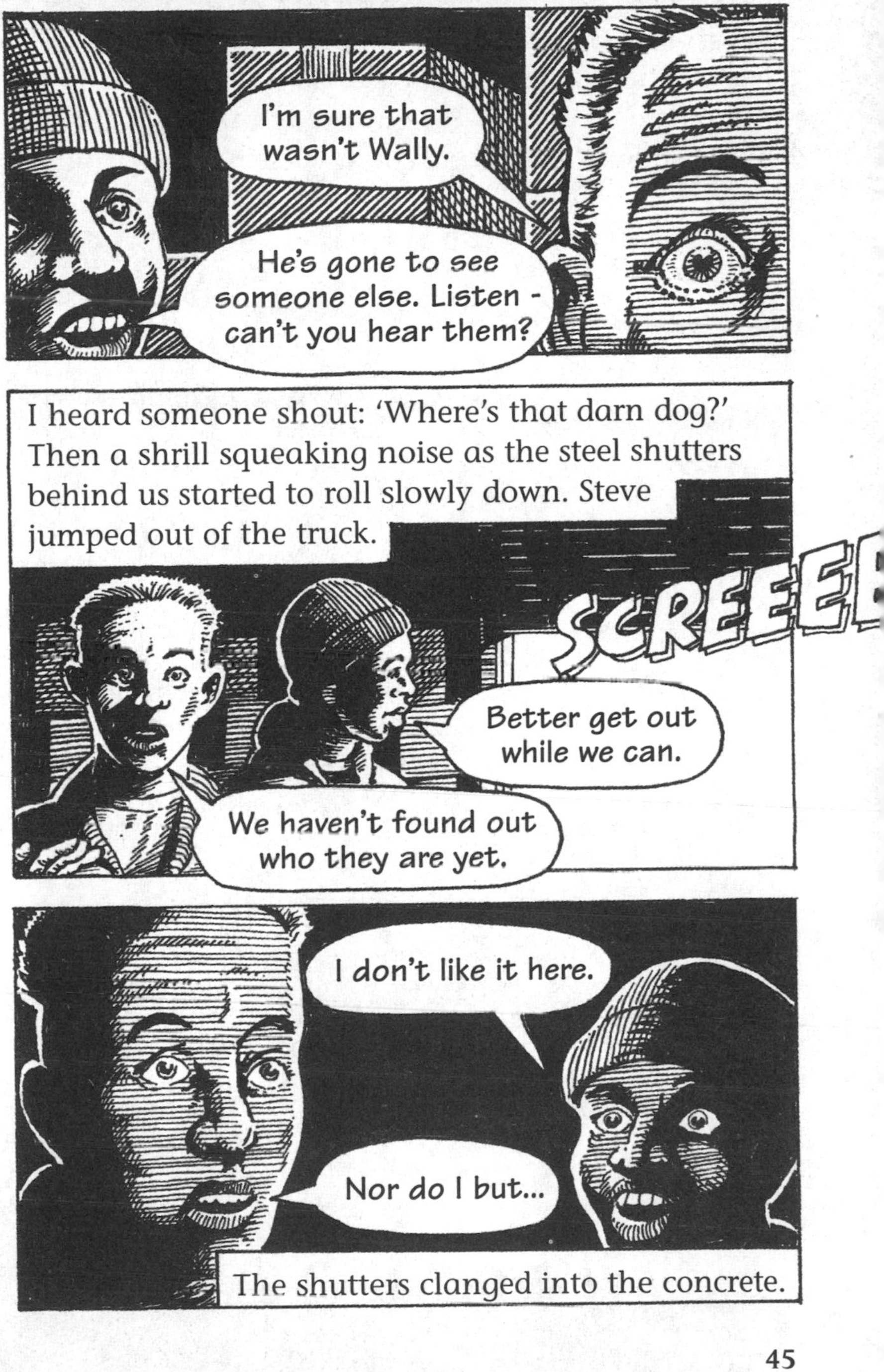
I'm sure that wasn't Wally.
He's gone to see someone else. Listen - can't you hear them?
I heard someone shout: 'Where's that darn dog?' Then a shrill squeaking noise as the steel shutters behind us started to roll slowly down. Steve jumped out of the truck.
SCREEE
Better get out while we can.
We haven't found out who they are yet.
I don't like it here.
Nor do I but...
The shutters clanged into the concrete.

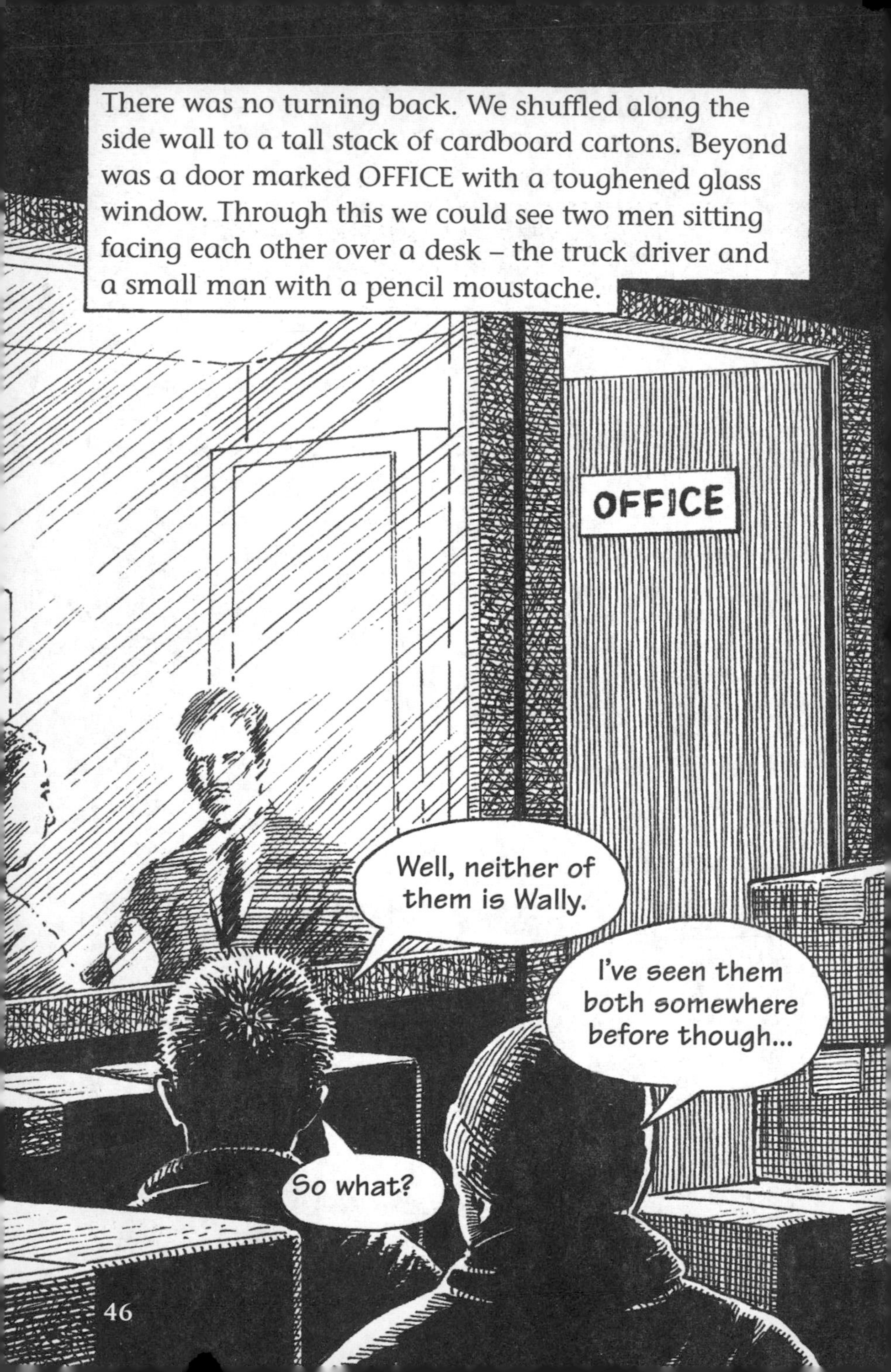
There was no turning back. We shuffled along the side wall to a tall stack of cardboard cartons. Beyond was a door marked OFFICE with a toughened glass window. Through this we could see two men sitting facing each other over a desk – the truck driver and a small man with a pencil moustache.
OFFICE
Well, neither of them is Wally.
I've seen them both somewhere before though...
So what?

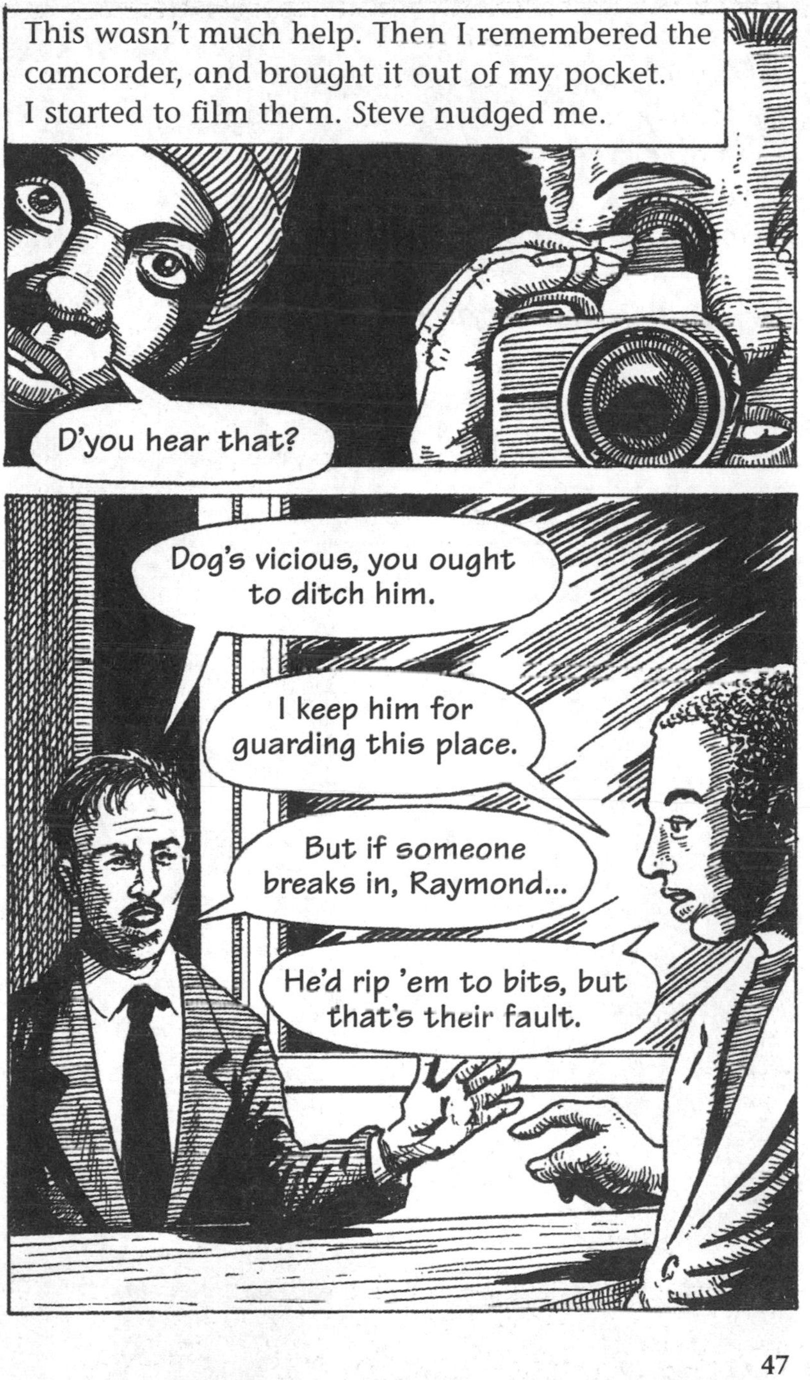
This wasn't much help. Then I remembered the camcorder, and brought it out of my pocket. I started to film them. Steve nudged me.
D'you hear that?
Dog's vicious, you ought to ditch him.
I keep him for guarding this place.
But if someone breaks in, Raymond...
He'd rip 'em to bits, but that's their fault.

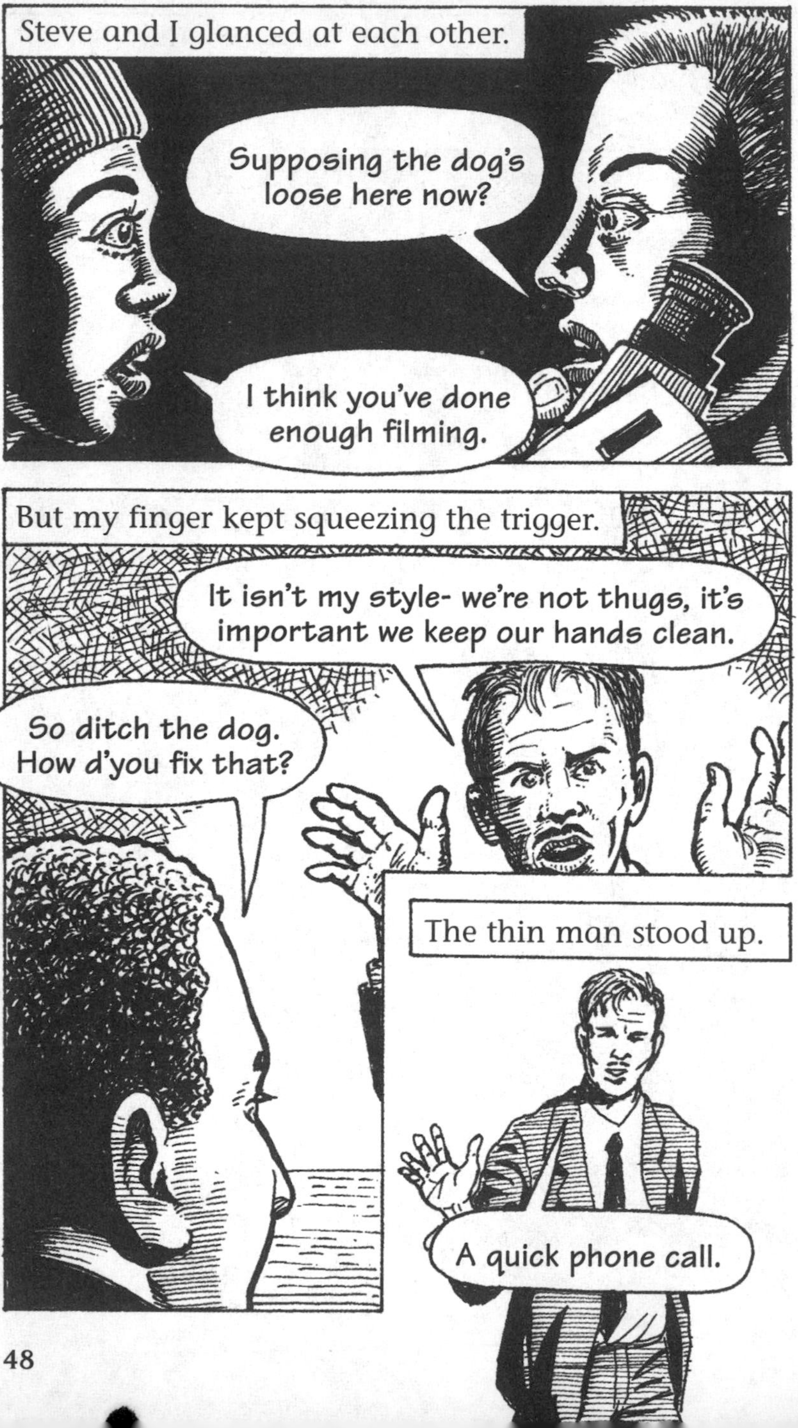
Steve and I glanced at each other.
Supposing the dog's loose here now?
I think you've done enough filming.
But my finger kept squeezing the trigger.
It isn't my style- we're not thugs, it's important we keep our hands clean.
So ditch the dog. How d'you fix that?
The thin man stood up.
A quick phone call.

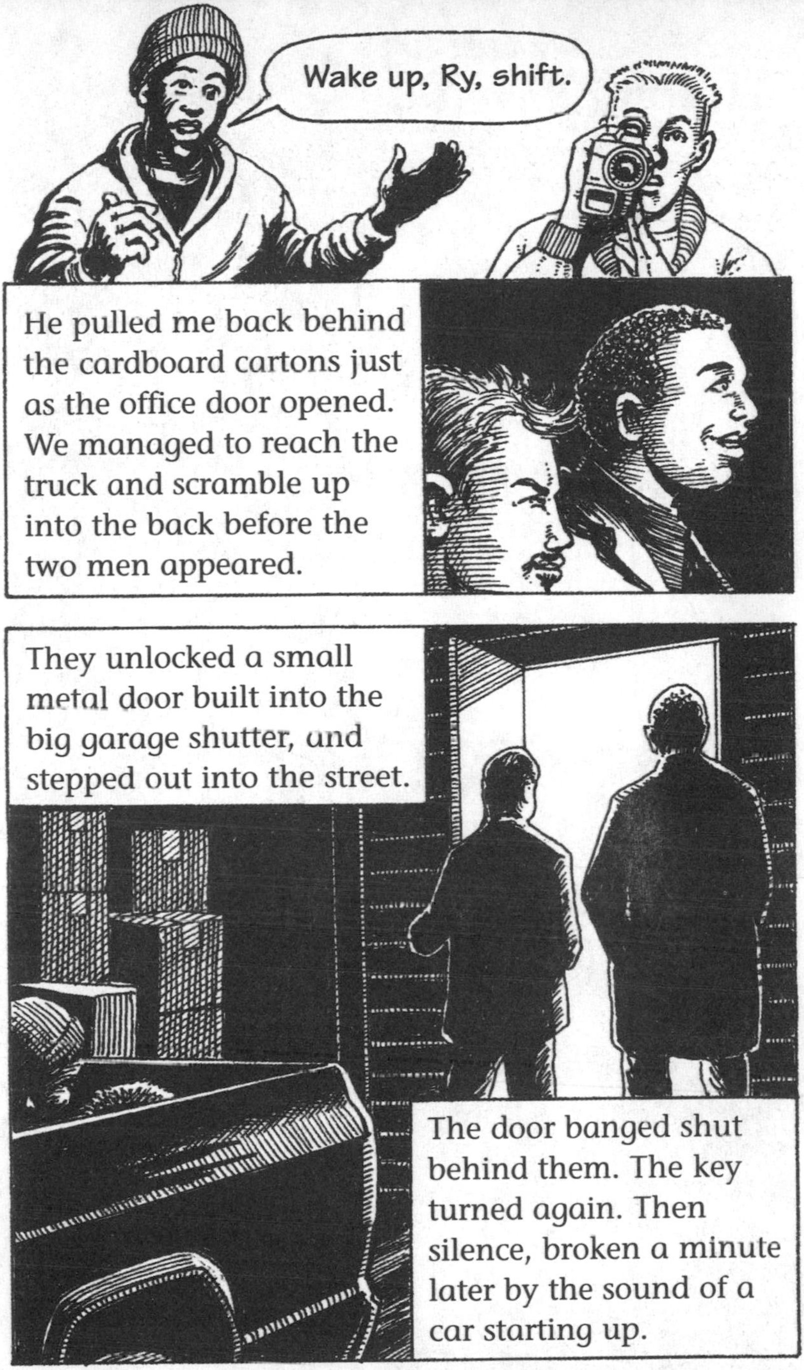
Wake up, Ry, shift.
He pulled me back behind the cardboard cartons just as the office door opened. We managed to reach the truck and scramble up into the back before the two men appeared.
They unlocked a small metal door built into the big garage shutter, and stepped out into the street.
The door banged shut behind them. The key turned again. Then silence, broken a minute later by the sound of a car starting up.

Chapter Seven

It was still only early evening, too soon for Mum or Dad to worry where I might have gone, and Steve said his mum and dad wouldn't be home until eight. By then Demon Den might have turned up to steal our car again, and even if Dad was waiting, he wouldn't have the camcorder to record the evidence.

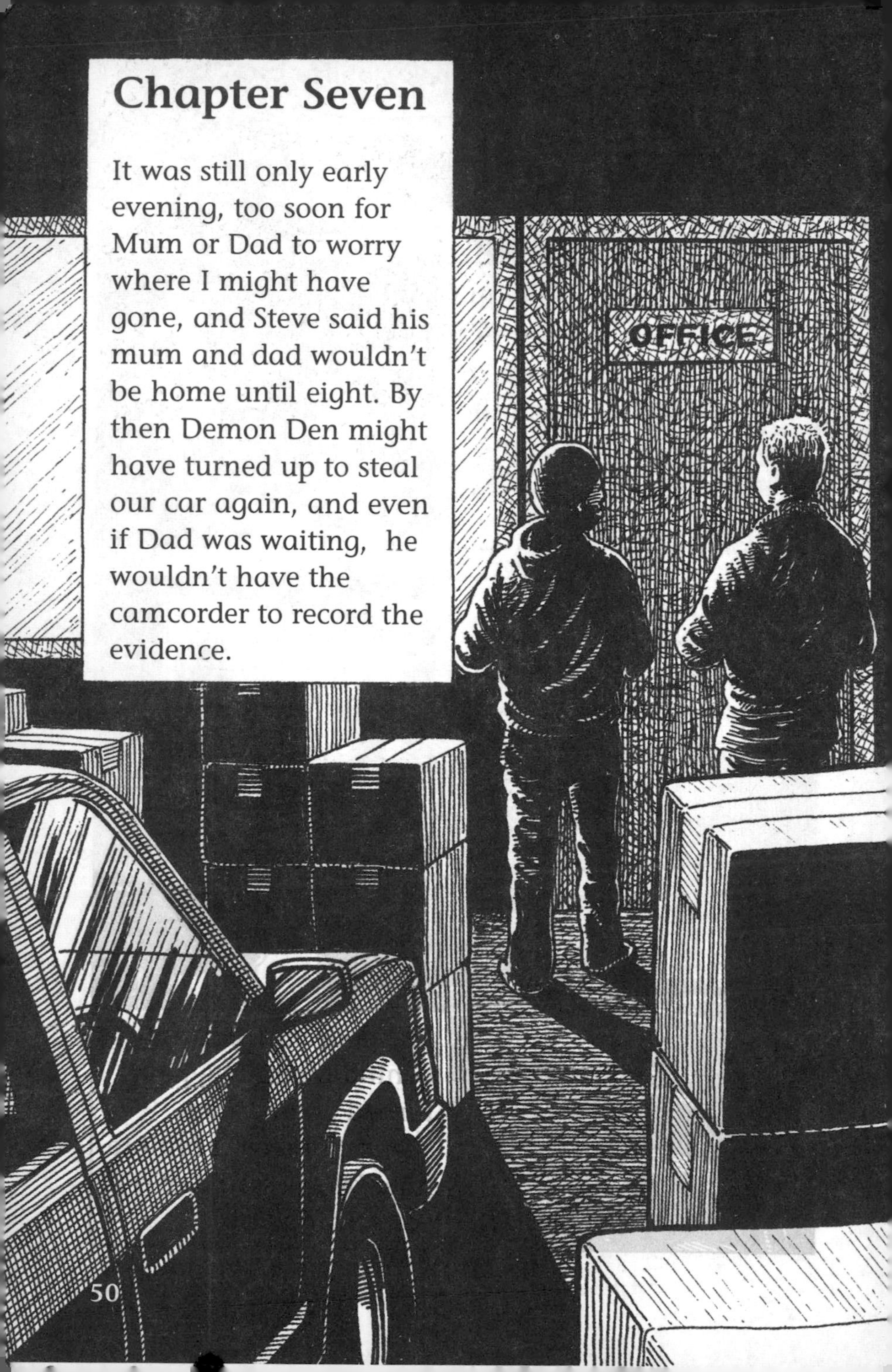
OFFICE

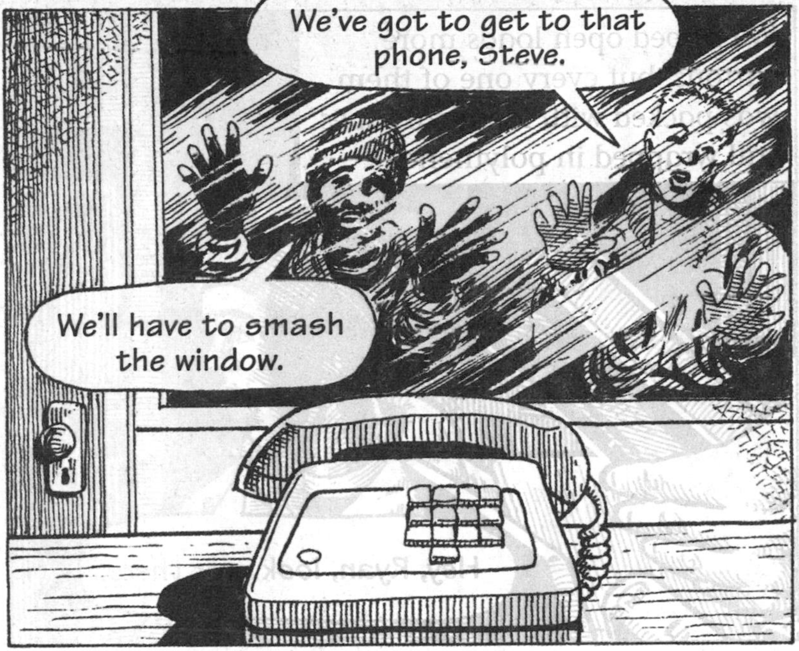
We've got to get to that phone, Steve.
We'll have to smash the window.

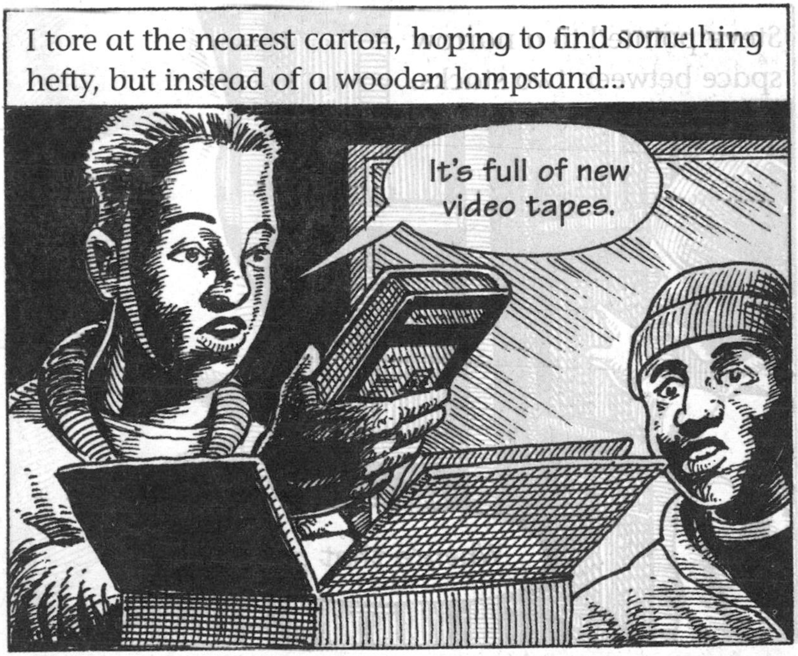
I tore at the nearest carton, hoping to find something hefty, but instead of a wooden lampstand...
It's full of new video tapes.

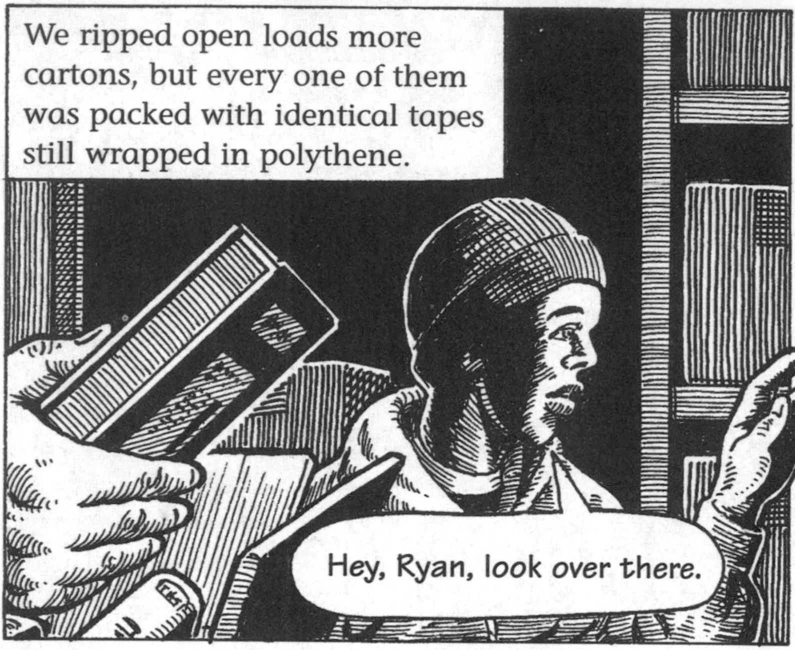
We ripped open loads more cartons, but every one of them was packed with identical tapes still wrapped in polythene.
Hey, Ryan, look over there.

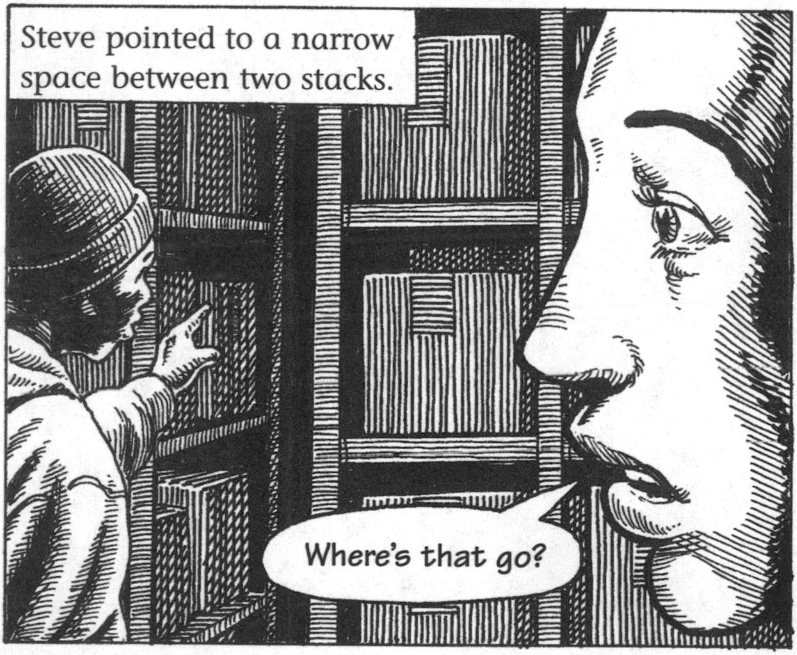
Steve pointed to a narrow space between two stacks.
Where's that go?

The space had been left as a passage, so people could reach the side wall where there was a low archway into the next vault. I let Steve take the lead.

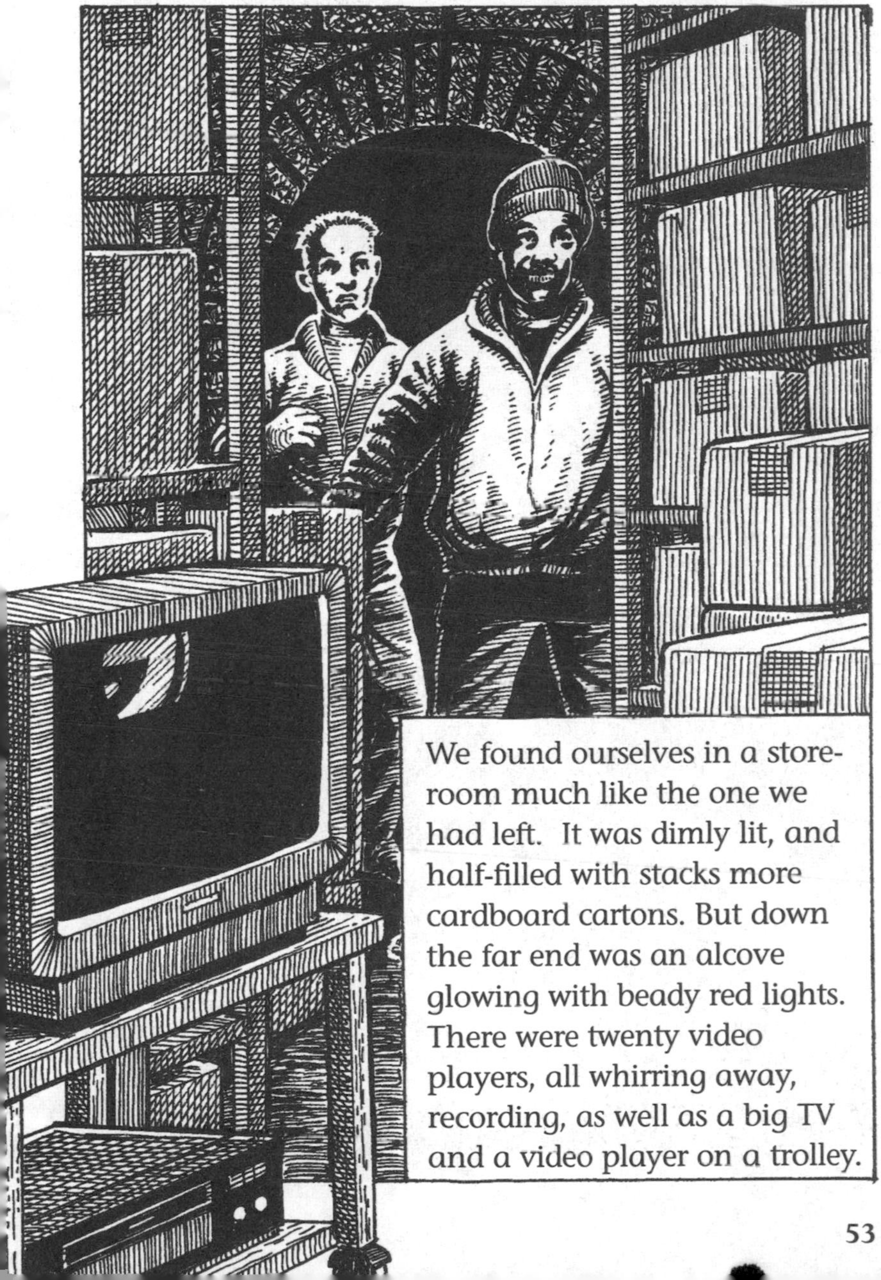

We found ourselves in a store-room much like the one we had left. It was dimly lit, and half-filled with stacks more cardboard cartons. But down the far end was an alcove glowing with beady red lights. There were twenty video players, all whirring away, recording, as well as a big TV and a video player on a trolley.

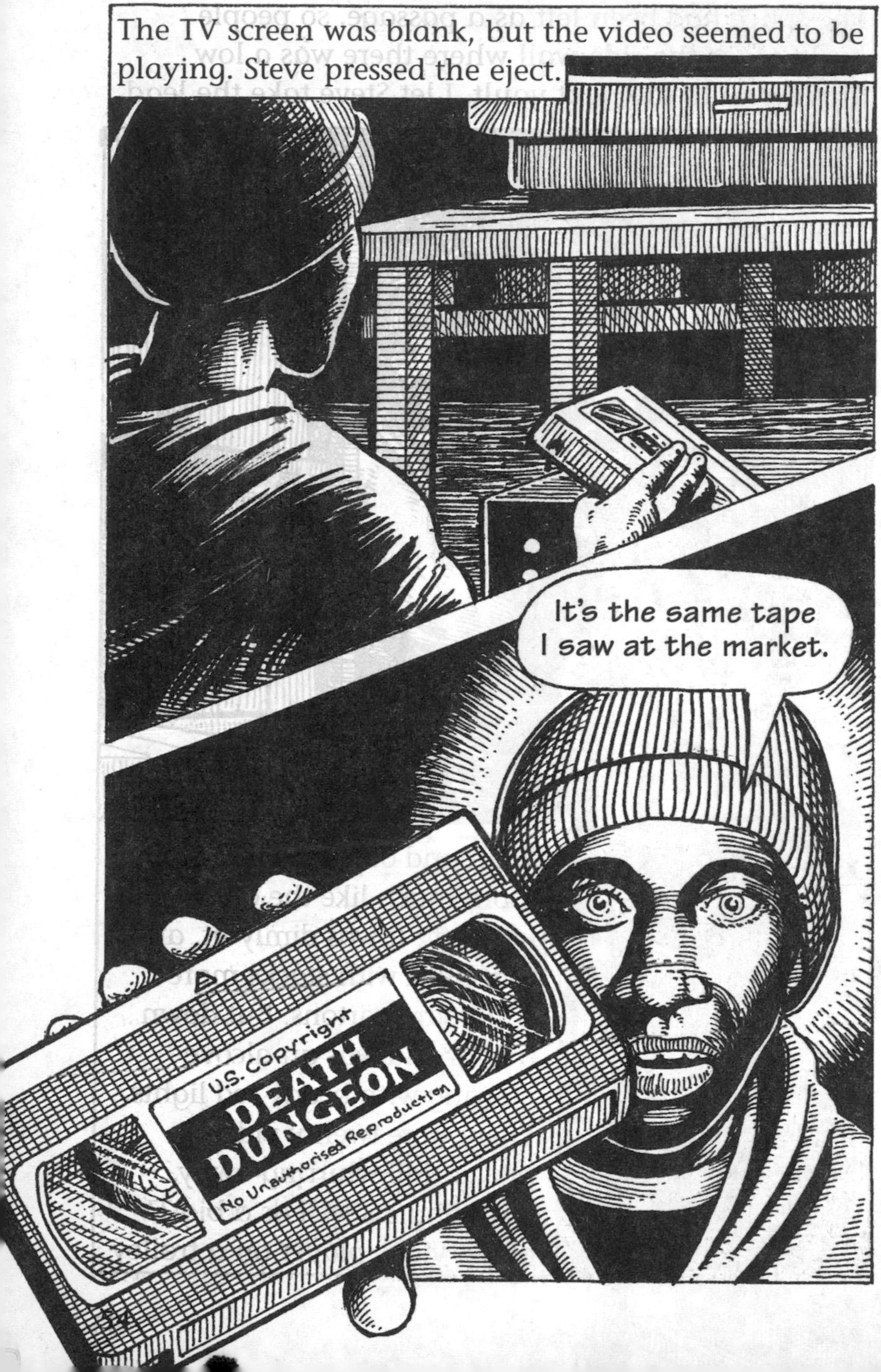
The TV screen was blank, but the video seemed to be playing. Steve pressed the eject.
It's the same tape I saw at the market.
U.S. Copyright
DEATH DUNGEON
No Unauthorised Reproduction

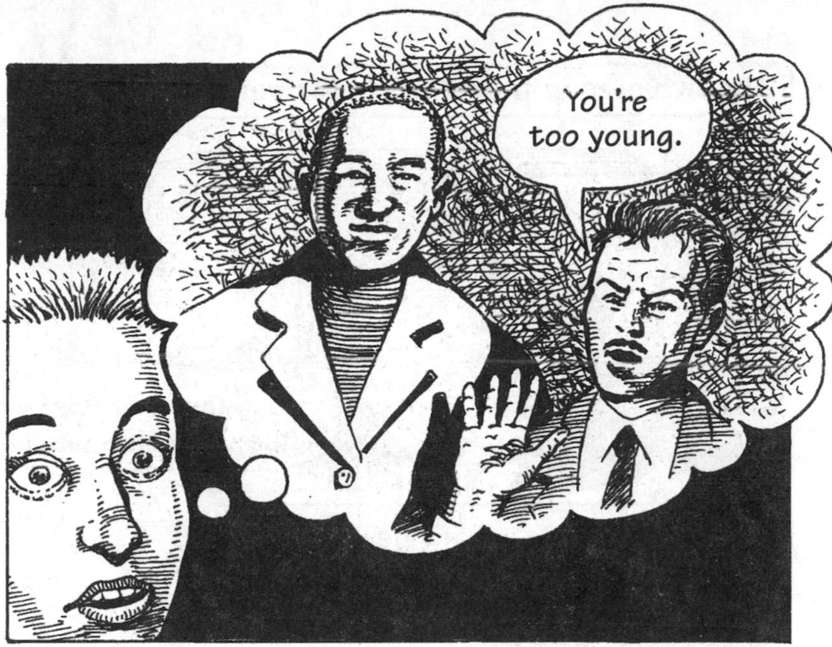
You're
too young.

I suddenly had an idea. Taking the tape from the camcorder, I plugged it into the player. I pressed rewind, then PLAY, and switched on the TV.

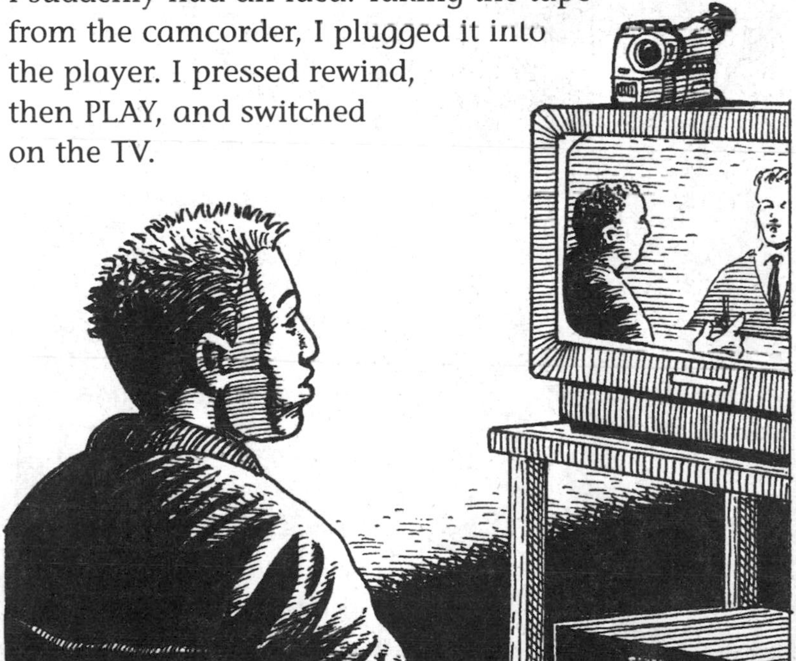

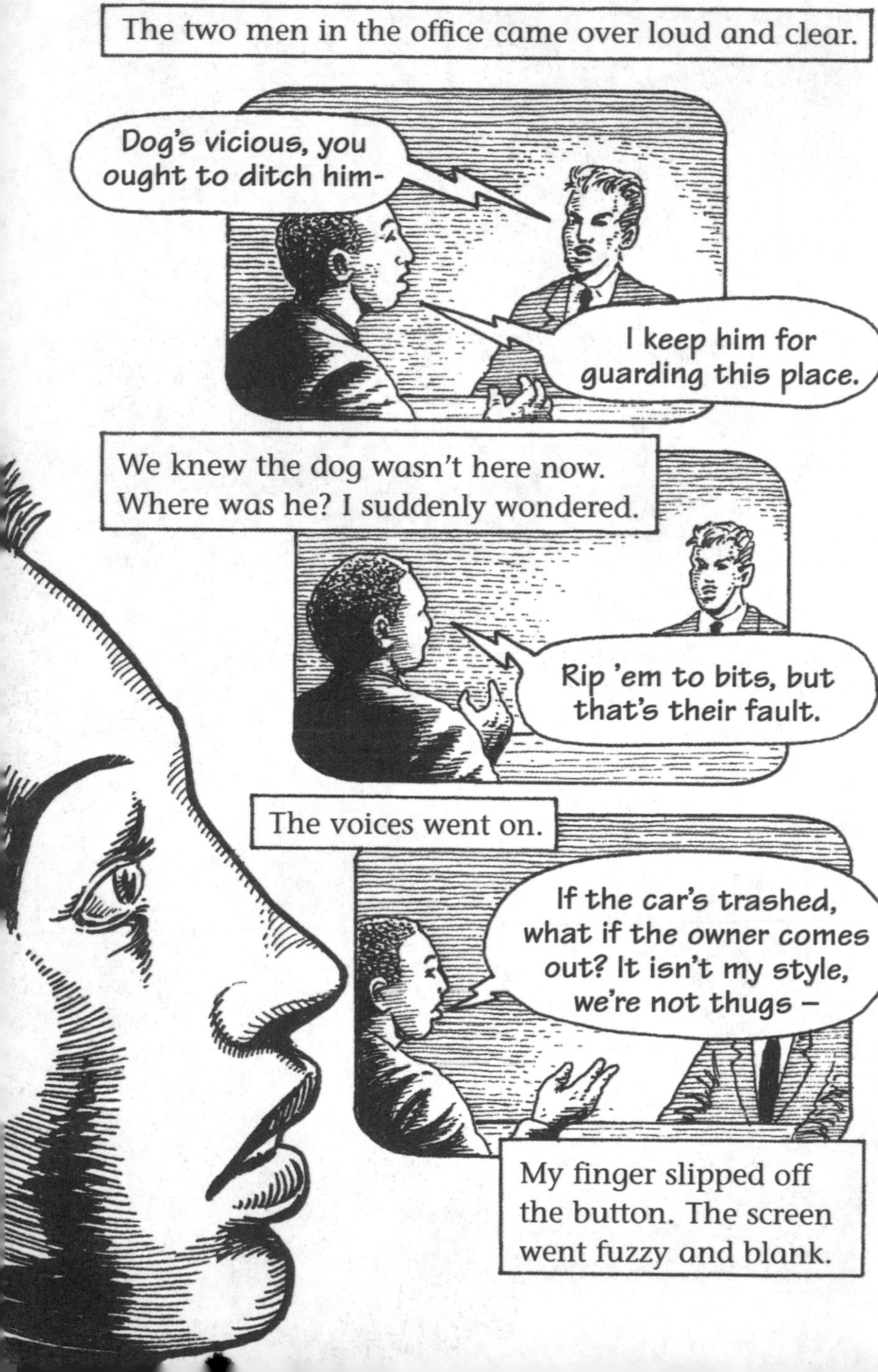
The two men in the office came over loud and clear.
Dog's vicious, you ought to ditch him-
I keep him for guarding this place.
We knew the dog wasn't here now. Where was he? I suddenly wondered.
Rip 'em to bits, but that's their fault.
The voices went on.
If the car's trashed, what if the owner comes out? It isn't my style, we're not thugs –
My finger slipped off the button. The screen went fuzzy and blank.

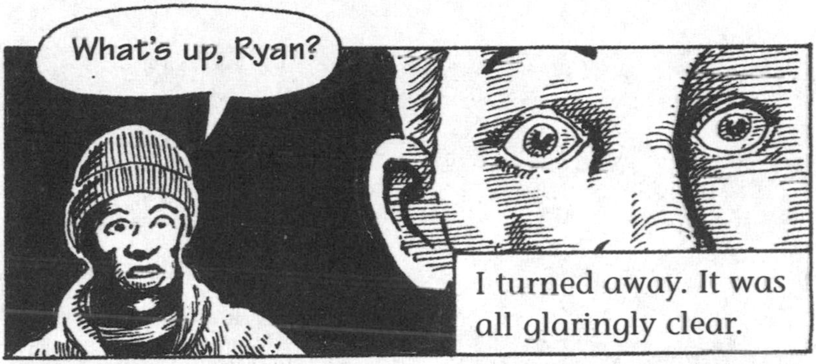
What's up, Ryan?
I turned away. It was all glaringly clear.

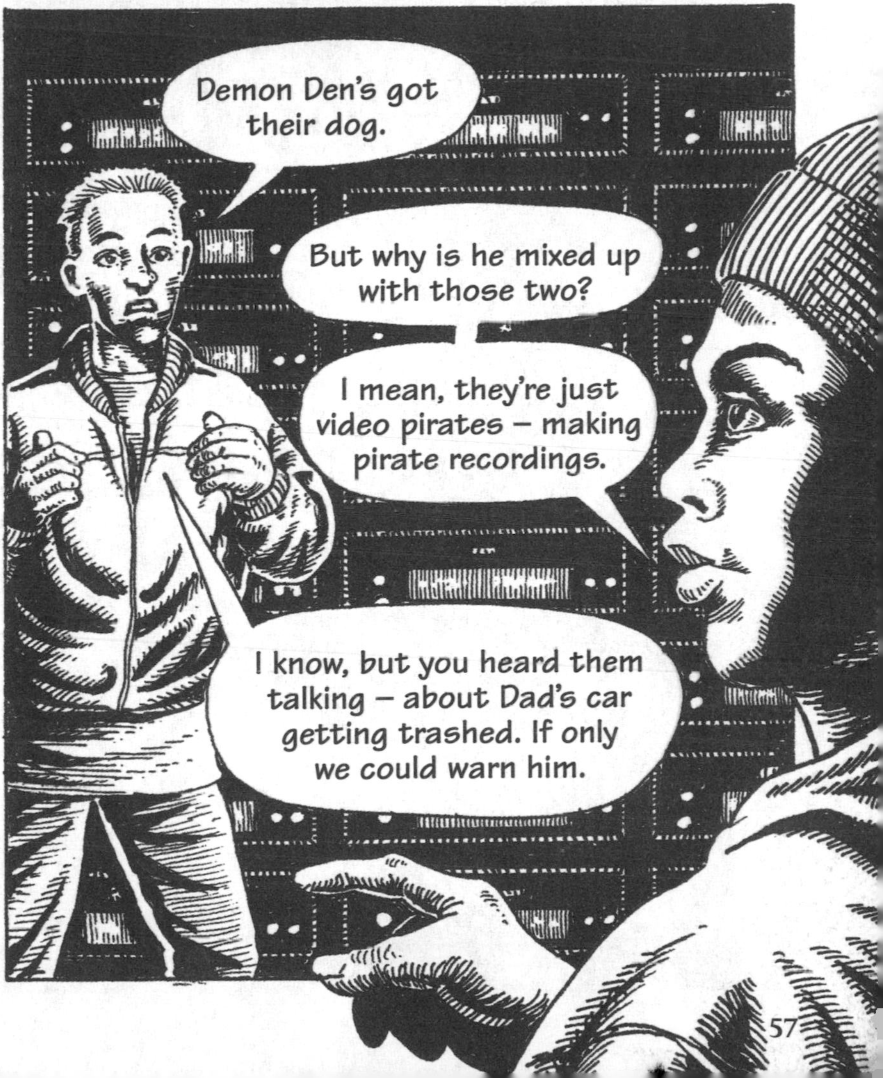
Demon Den's got their dog.
But why is he mixed up with those two?
I mean, they're just video pirates – making pirate recordings.
I know, but you heard them talking – about Dad's car getting trashed. If only we could warn him.

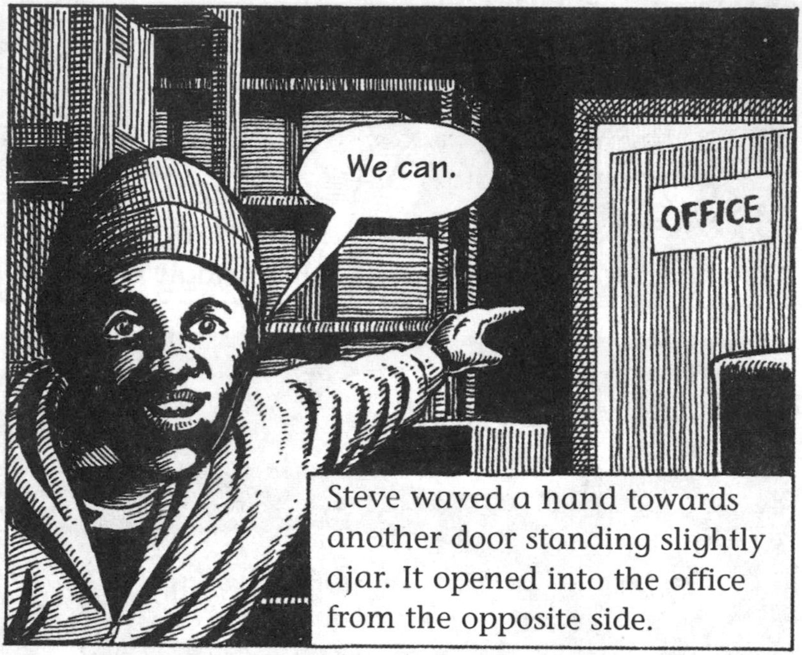
We can.
Steve waved a hand towards another door standing slightly ajar. It opened into the office from the opposite side.
OFFICE

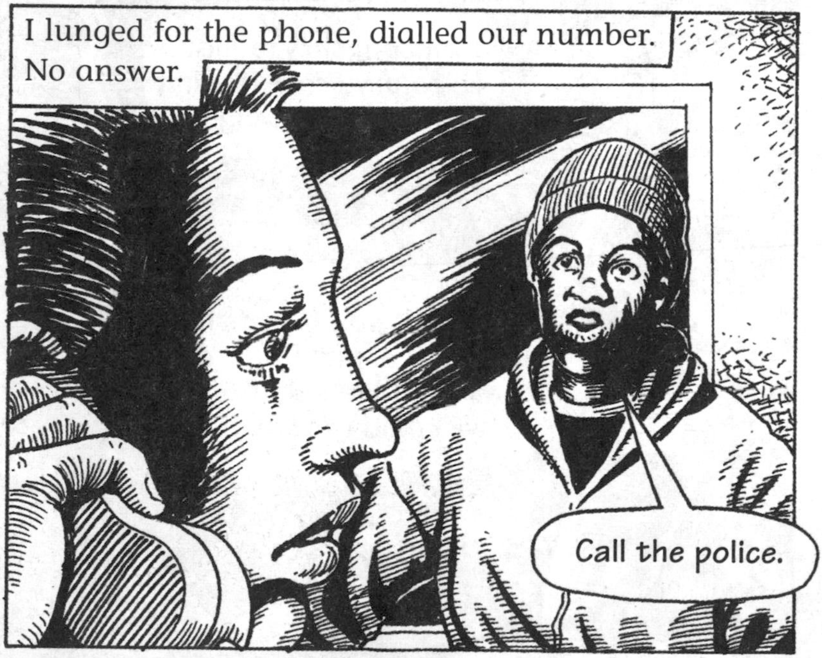
I lunged for the phone, dialled our number. No answer.
Call the police.

I wavered, thinking fast. Demon D must have taken Dad's car to help the video pirates get Dad's place at the market. If Wally had sold Dad's lampstands he might have bought them from Demon without knowing where they had come from. If so, we'd got it wrong about the D standing for Den. Demon D was NOT Wally's partner. And Wally was not a crook.

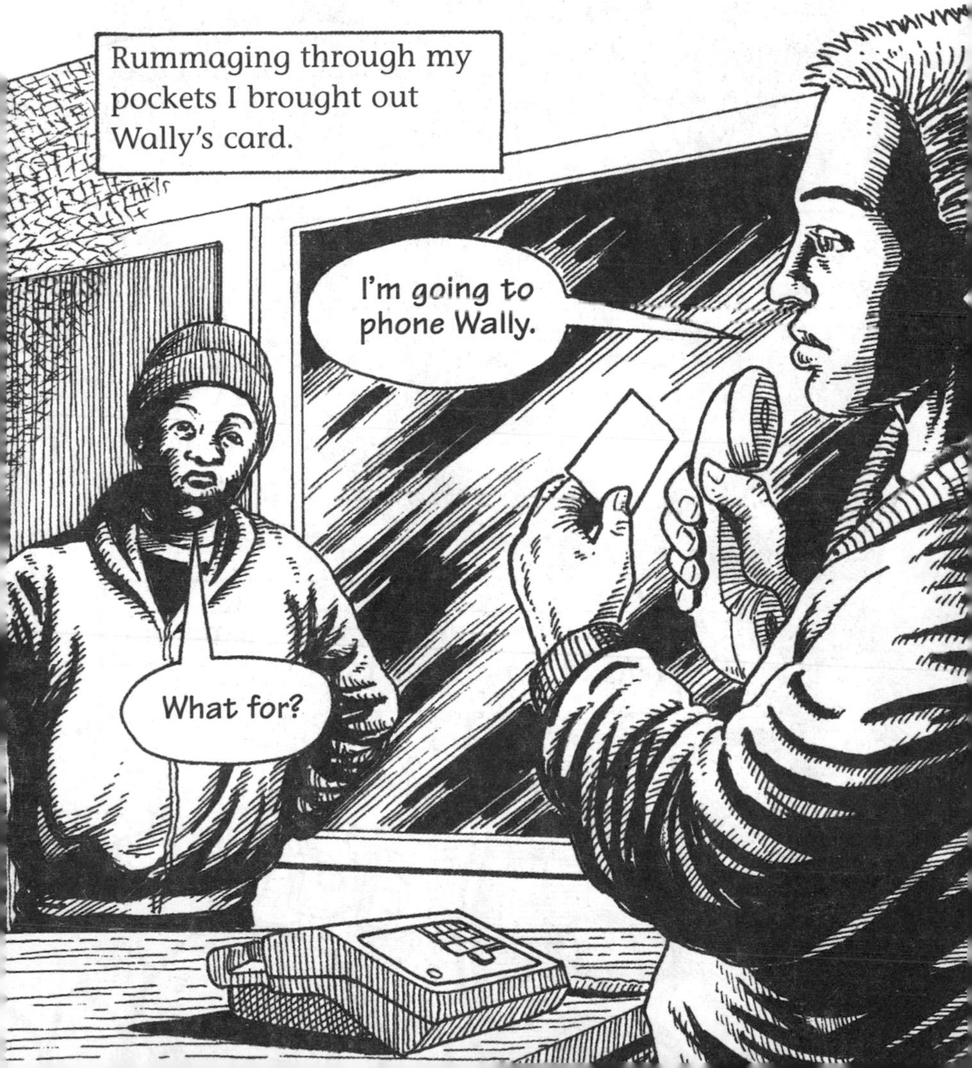
Rummaging through my pockets I brought out Wally's card.
I'm going to phone Wally.
What for?

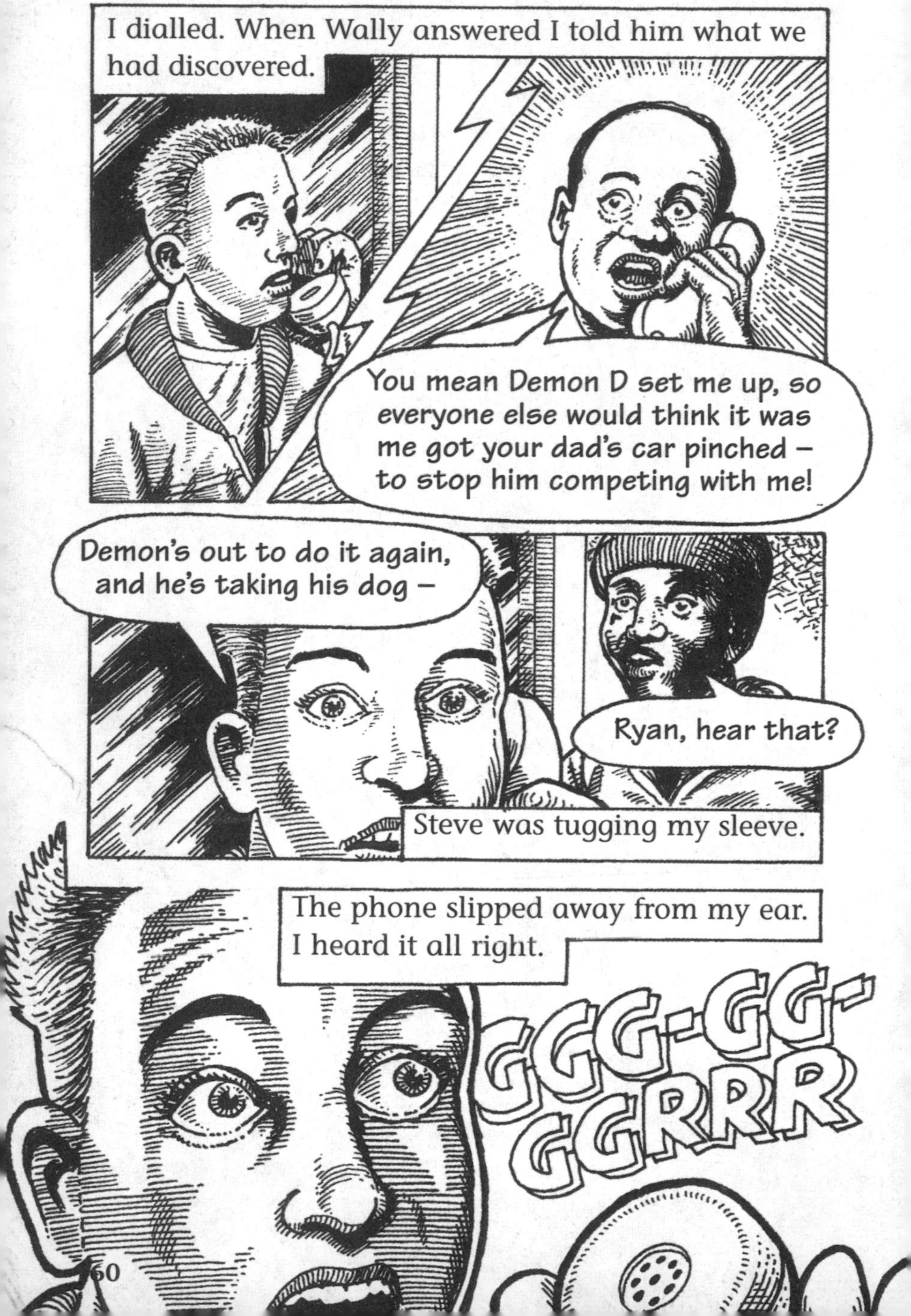
I dialled. When Wally answered I told him what we had discovered.
You mean Demon D set me up, so everyone else would think it was me got your dad's car pinched – to stop him competing with me!
Demon's out to do it again, and he's taking his dog –
Ryan, hear that?
Steve was tugging my sleeve.
The phone slipped away from my ear. I heard it all right.
GGG-GG-GGRRR

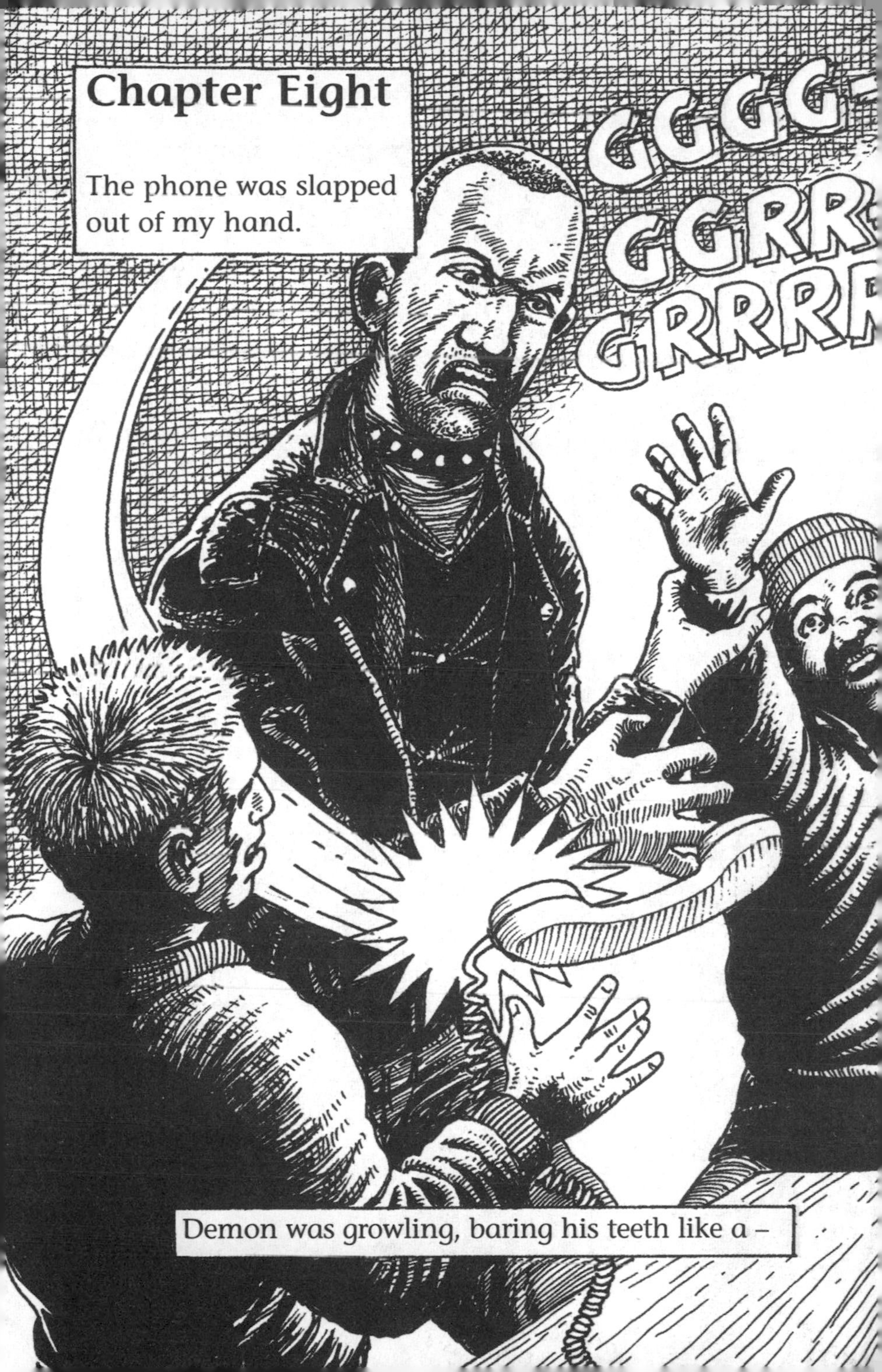
Chapter Eight
The phone was slapped out of my hand.
GGGG-
GGRR
GRRRR
Demon was growling, baring his teeth like a –

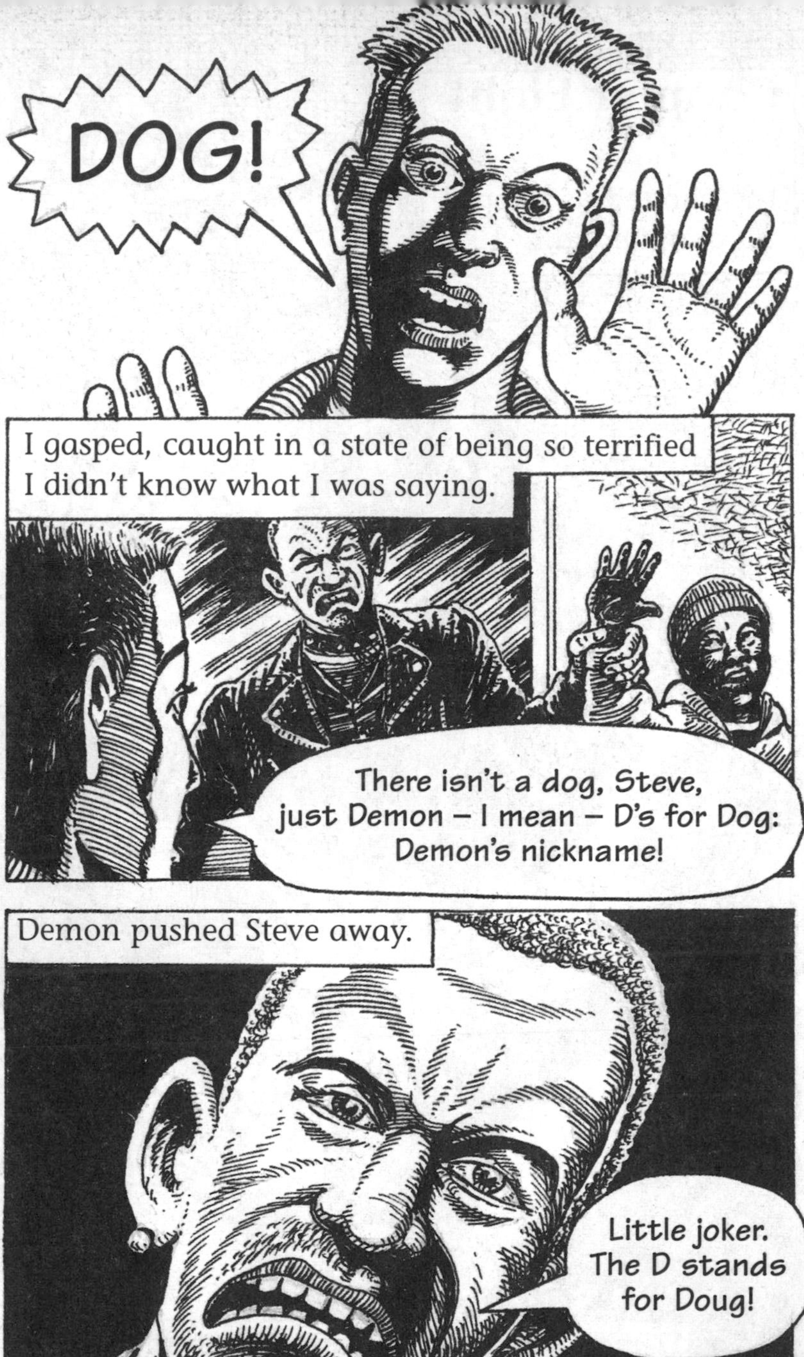
DOG!
I gasped, caught in a state of being so terrified I didn't know what I was saying.
There isn't a dog, Steve, just Demon – I mean – D's for Dog: Demon's nickname!
Demon pushed Steve away.
Little joker. The D stands for Doug!

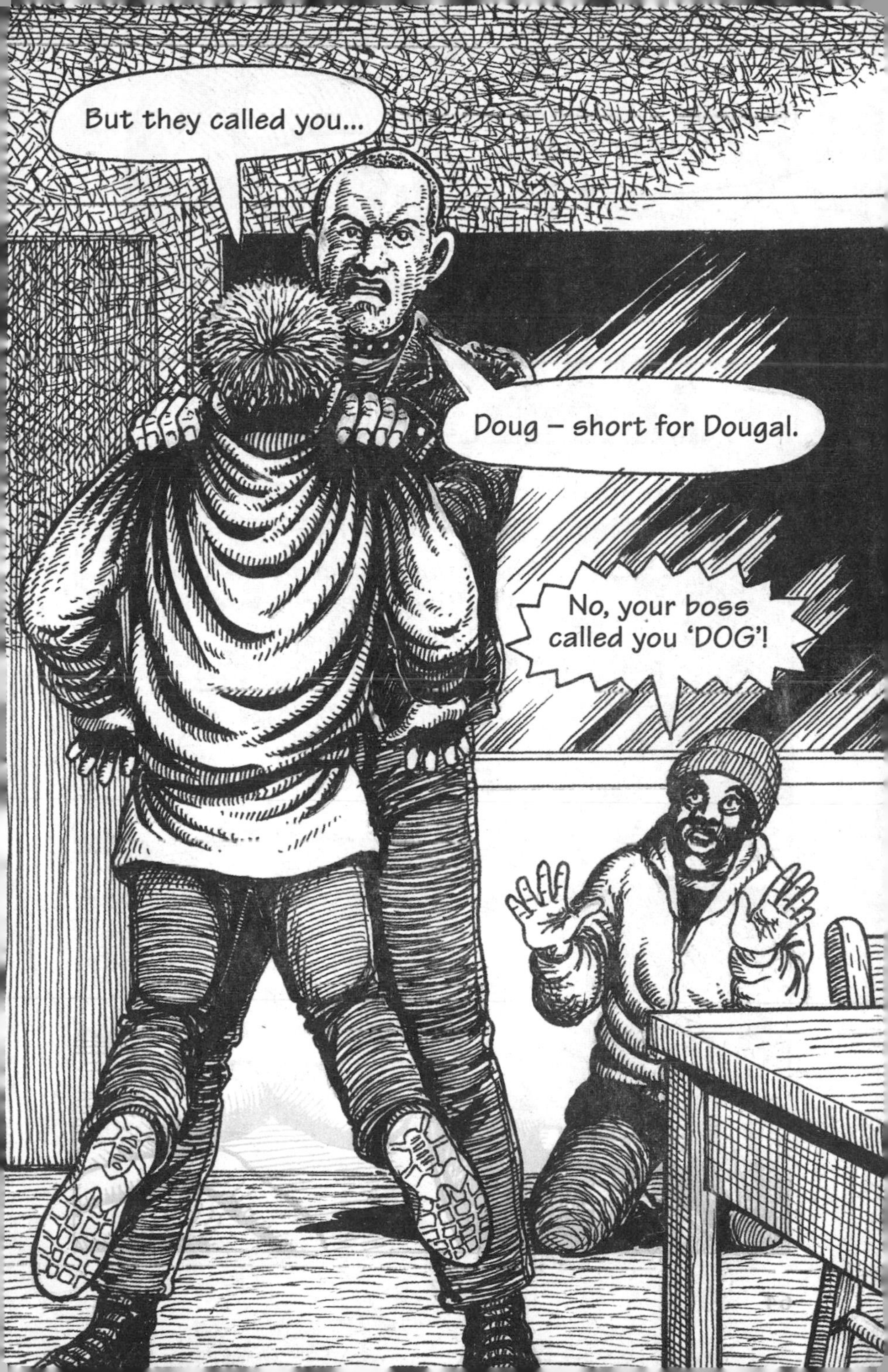
But they called you...
Doug – short for Dougal.
No, your boss called you 'DOG'!

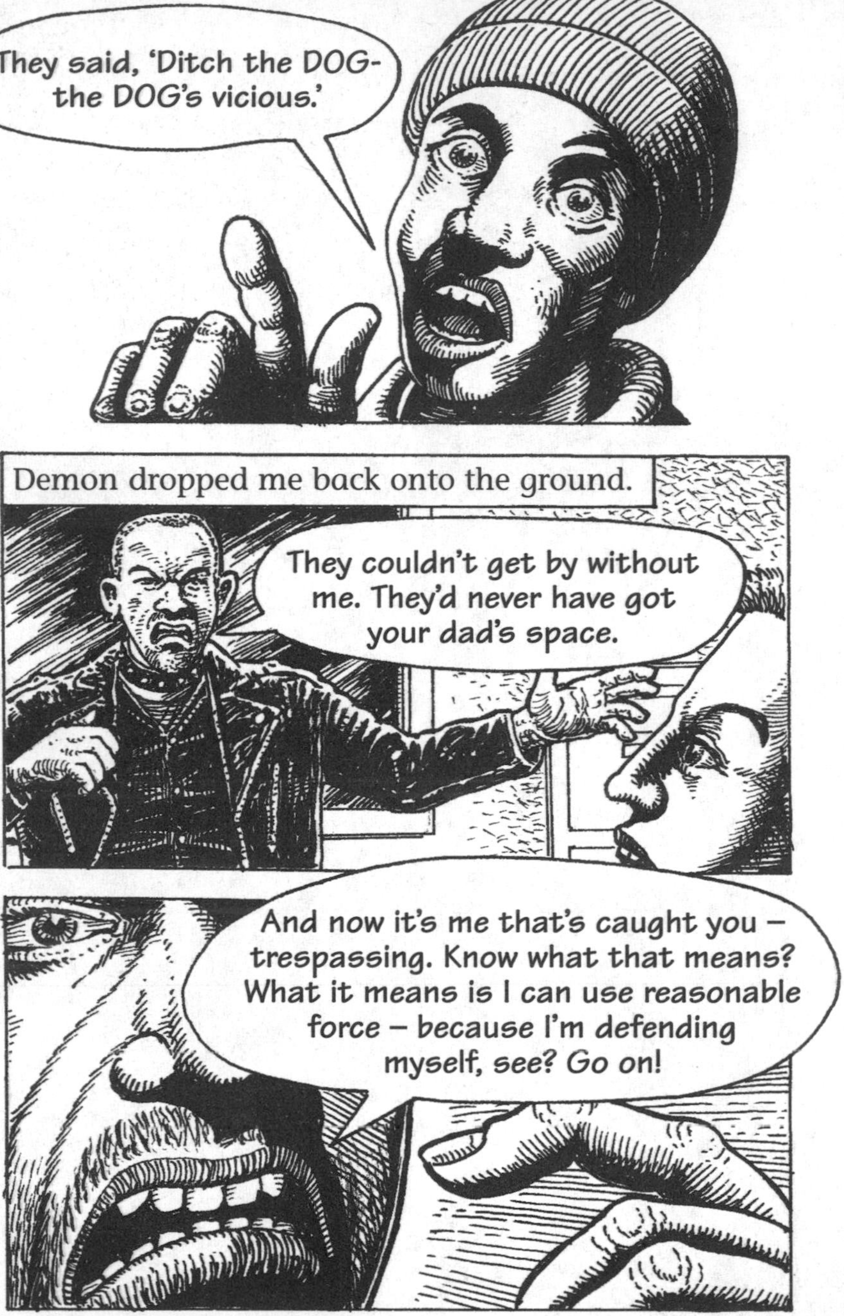
They said, 'Ditch the DOG- the DOG's vicious.'
Demon dropped me back onto the ground.
They couldn't get by without me. They'd never have got your dad's space.
And now it's me that's caught you – trespassing. Know what that means? What it means is I can use reasonable force – because I'm defending myself, see? Go on!

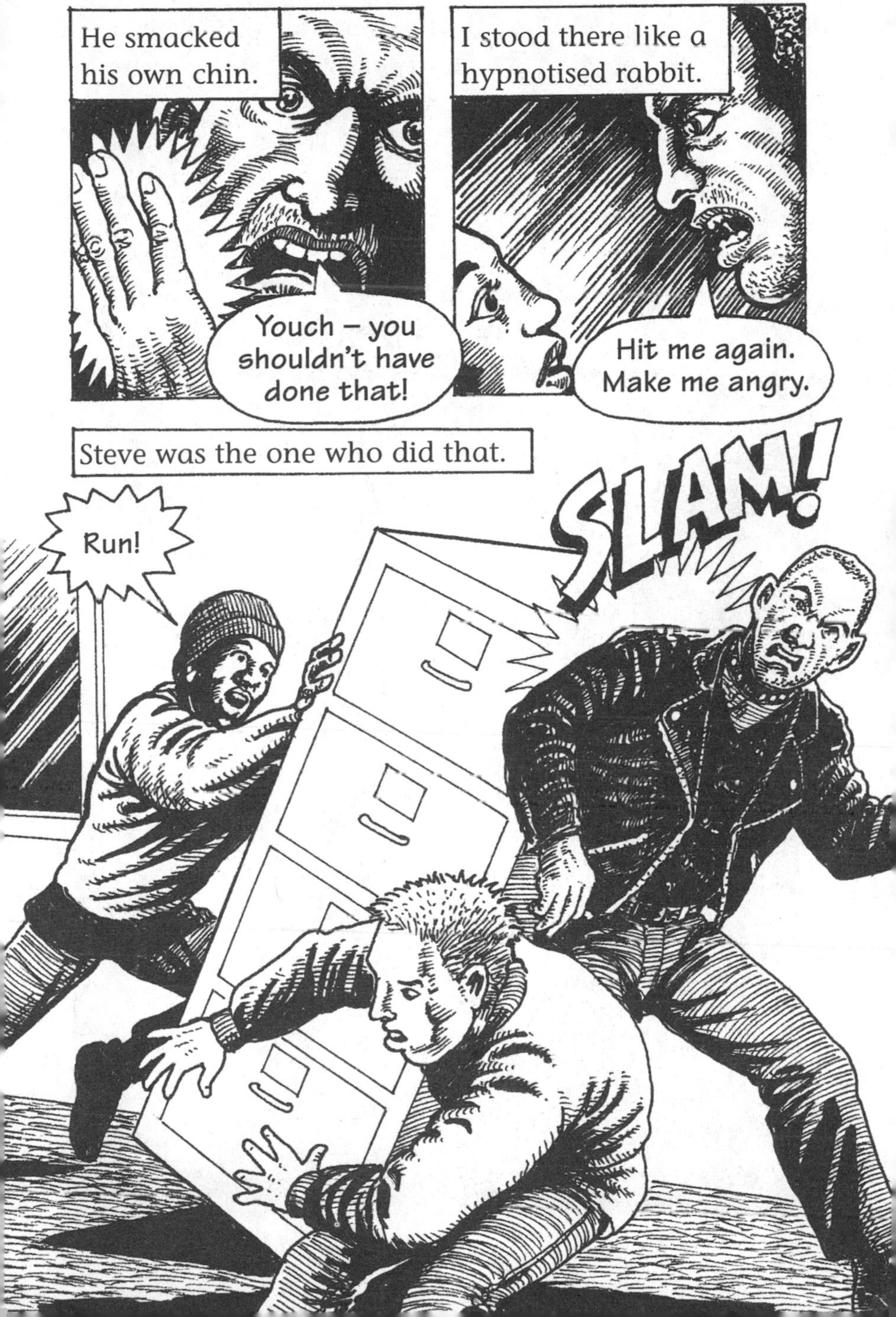
He smacked his own chin.
Youch – you shouldn't have done that!
I stood there like a hypnotised rabbit.
Hit me again. Make me angry.
Steve was the one who did that.
Run!
SLAM!

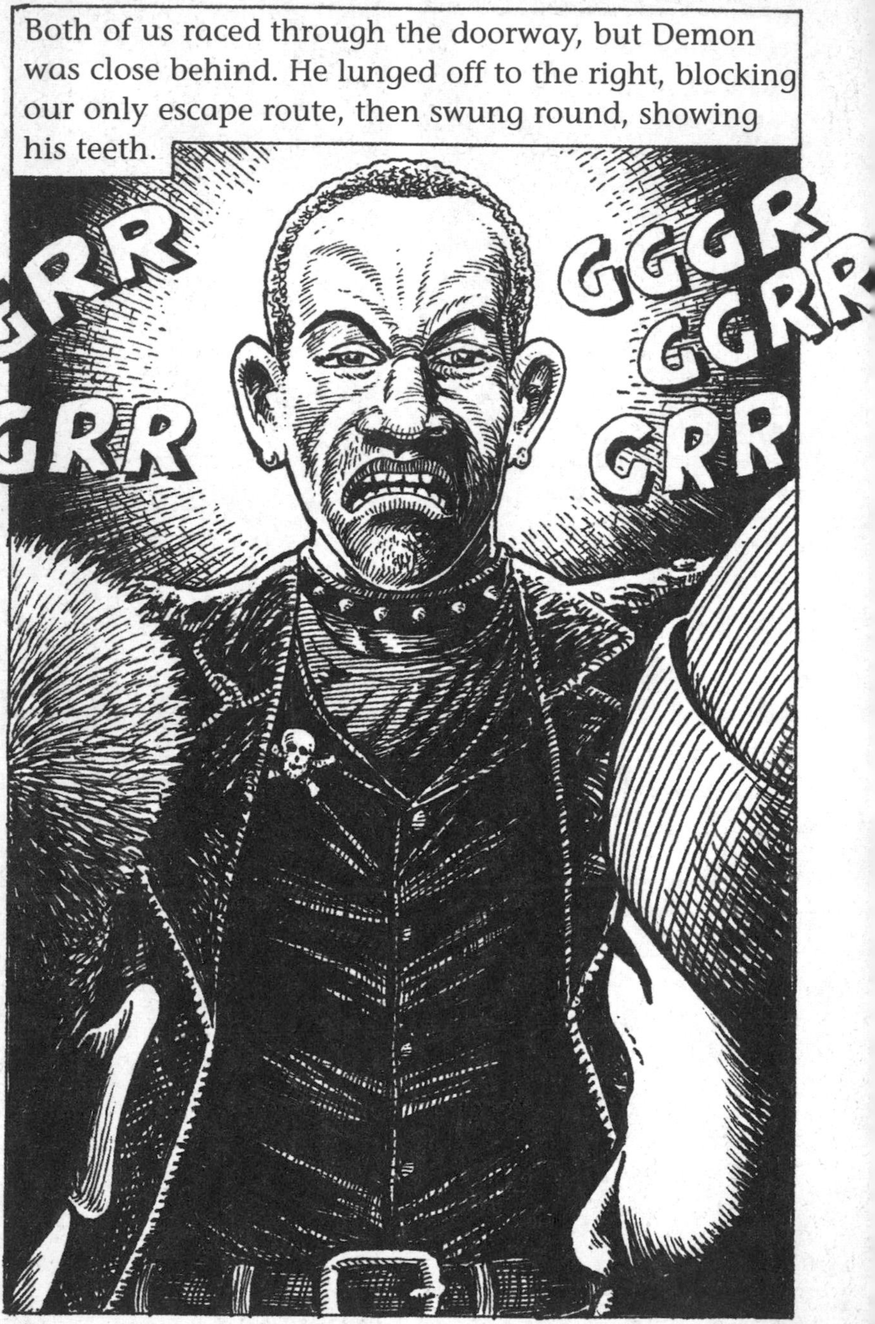
Both of us raced through the doorway, but Demon was close behind. He lunged off to the right, blocking our only escape route, then swung round, showing his teeth.
GRR
GRR
GGGR
GGRR
GRR

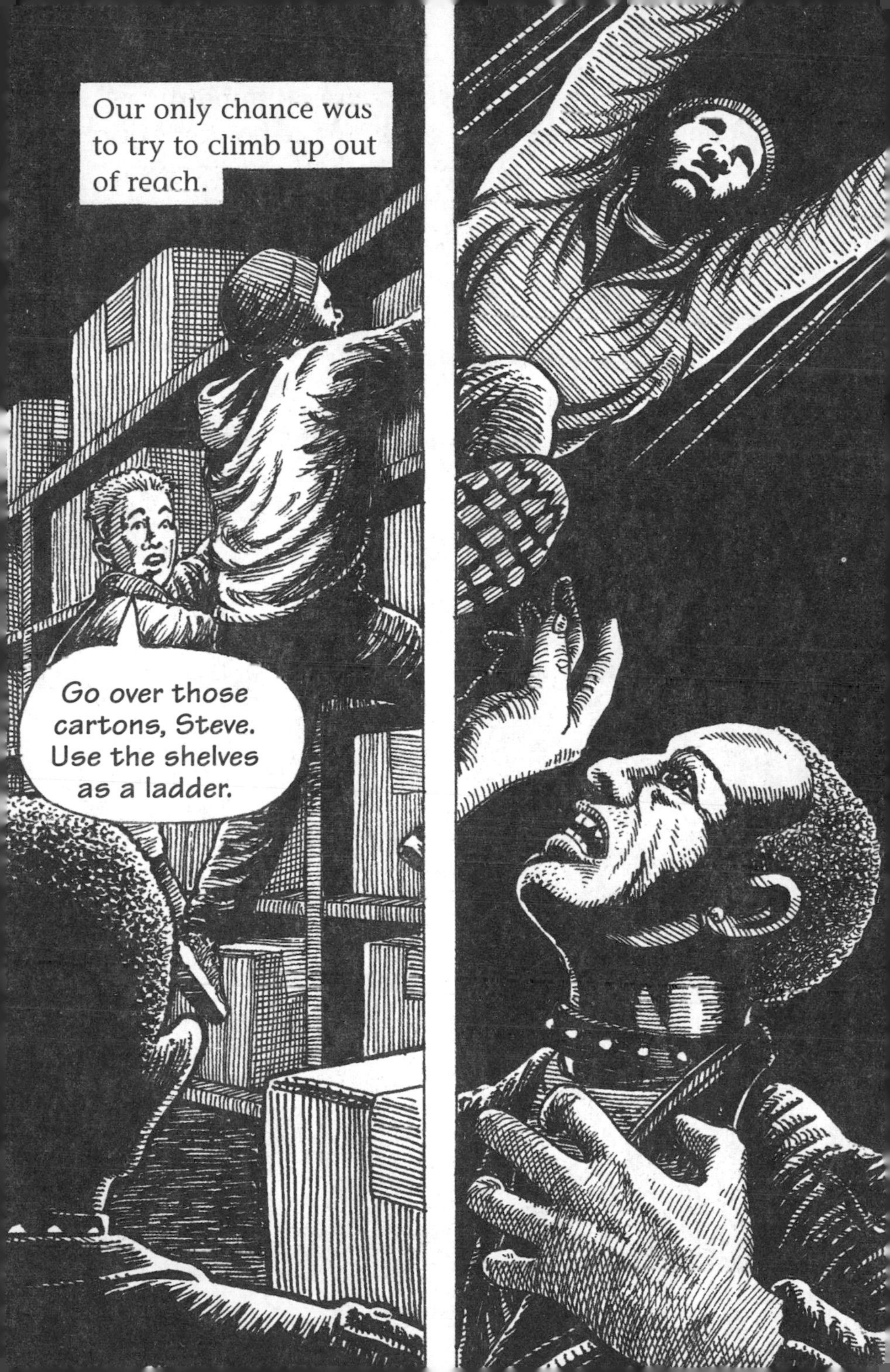
Our only chance was to try to climb up out of reach.
Go over those cartons, Steve. Use the shelves as a ladder.

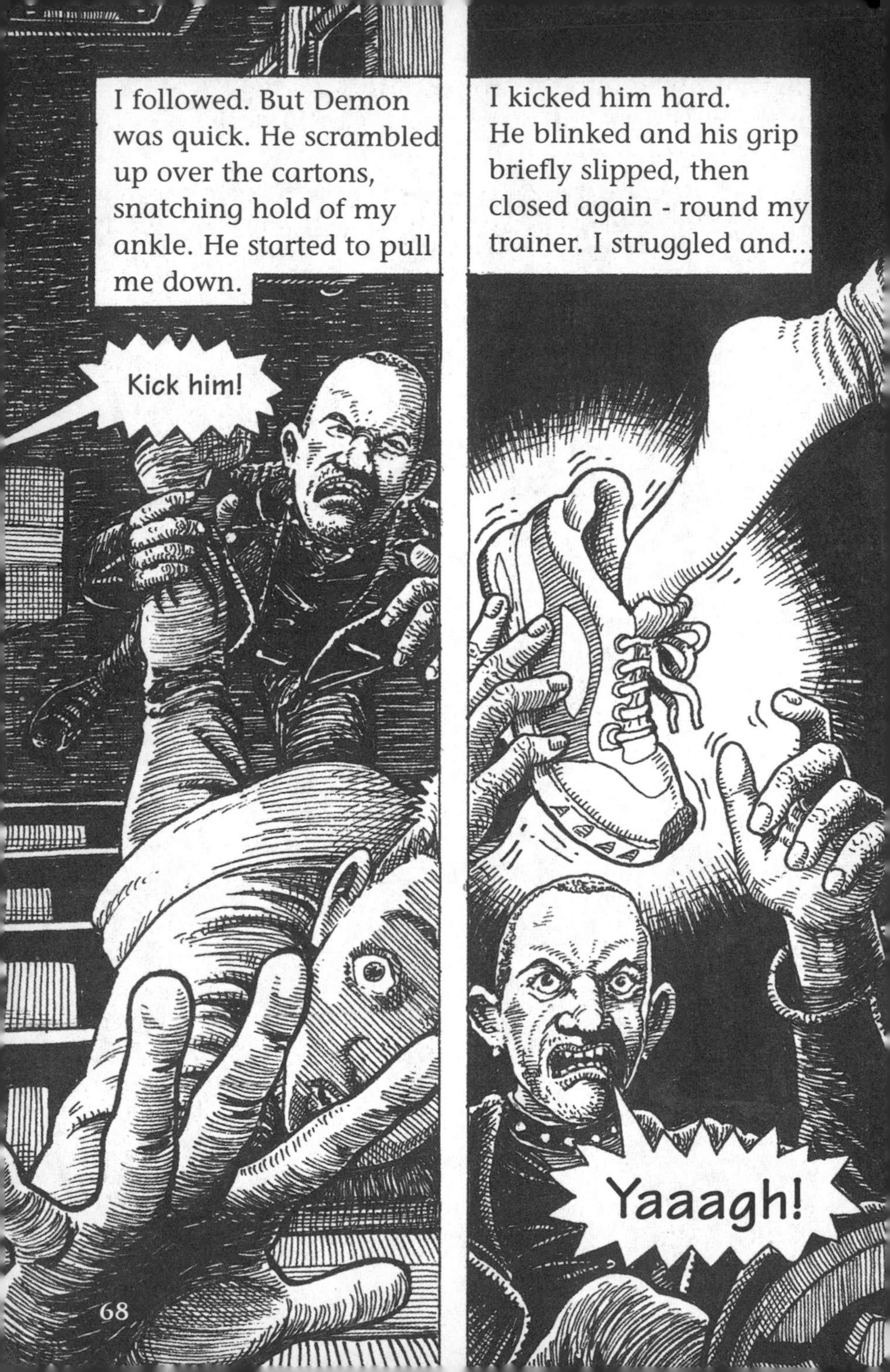
I followed. But Demon was quick. He scrambled up over the cartons, snatching hold of my ankle. He started to pull me down.
Kick him!
I kicked him hard. He blinked and his grip briefly slipped, then closed again - round my trainer. I struggled and...
Yaaagh!

He whammed into the trolley, knocking the video player and somehow switching it on. He stared at the screen in amazement.

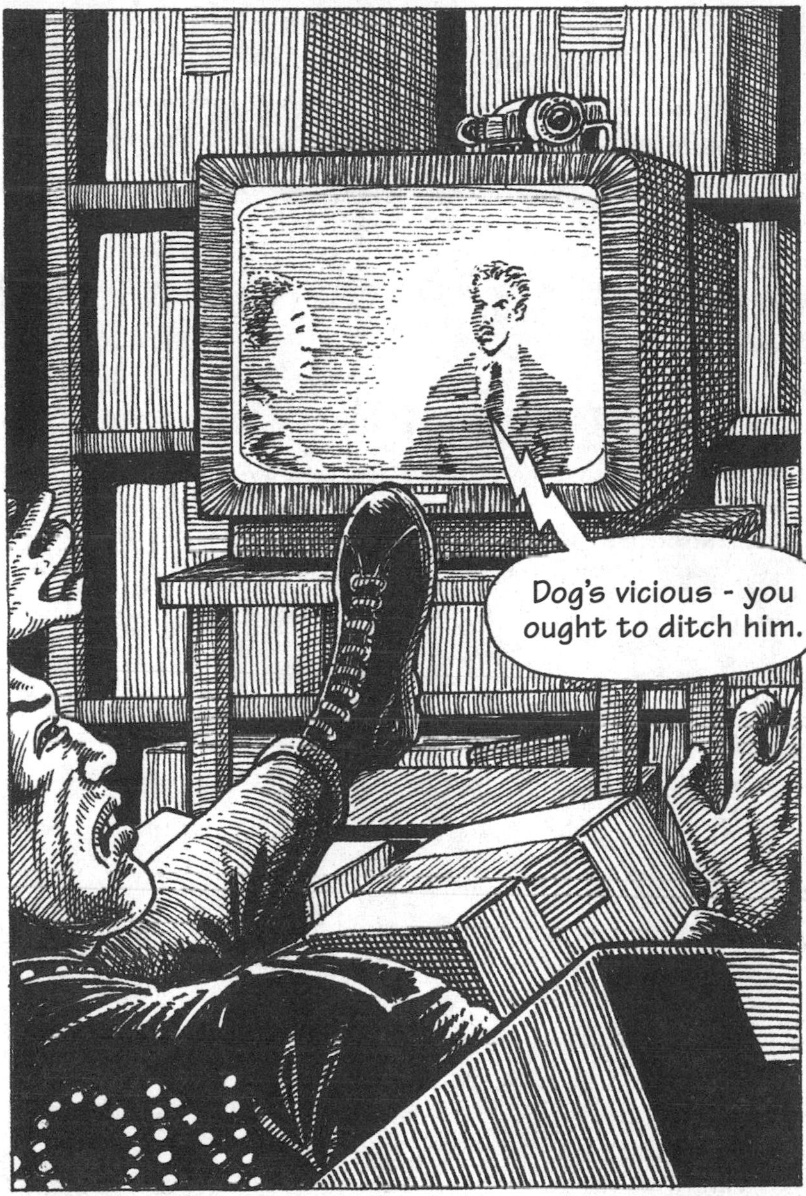
Dog's vicious - you ought to ditch him.

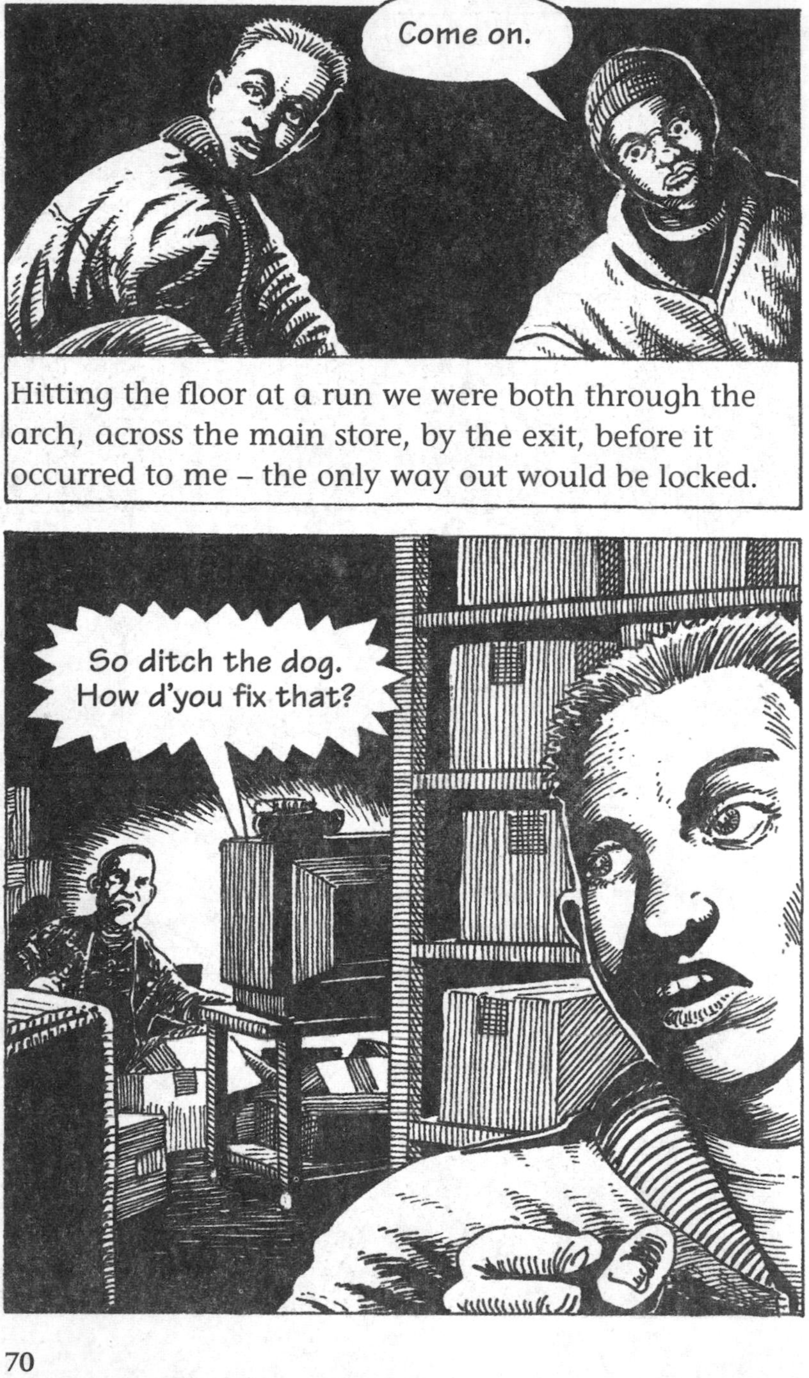
Come on.
Hitting the floor at a run we were both through the arch, across the main store, by the exit, before it occurred to me – the only way out would be locked.
So ditch the dog. How d'you fix that?

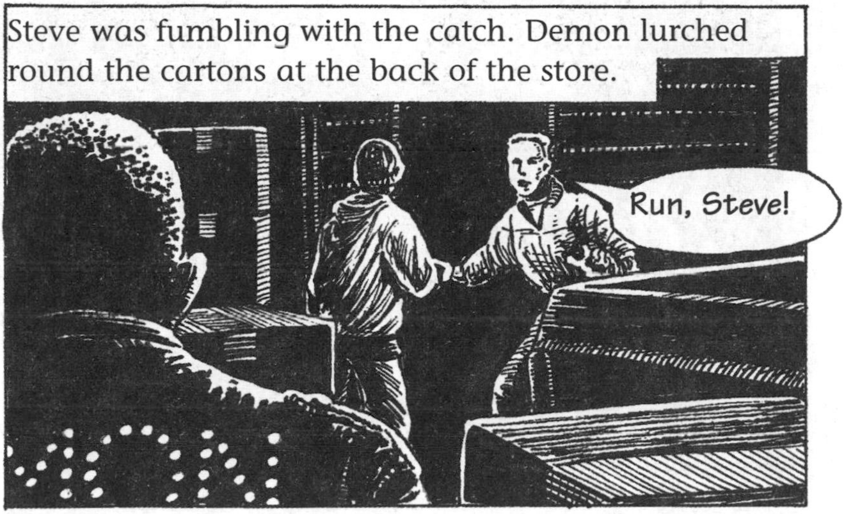
Steve was fumbling with the catch. Demon lurched round the cartons at the back of the store.
Run, Steve!

We dodged round behind the pick-up, but there was nowhere to hide. I thought this was it – he'd get us, then go off and trash Dad's car, and if Dad was there Dad would get trashed. I'd really mucked everything up. But Demon strode straight to the door, drilled a key in the lock and stumbled out into the street, leaving the door swinging open.

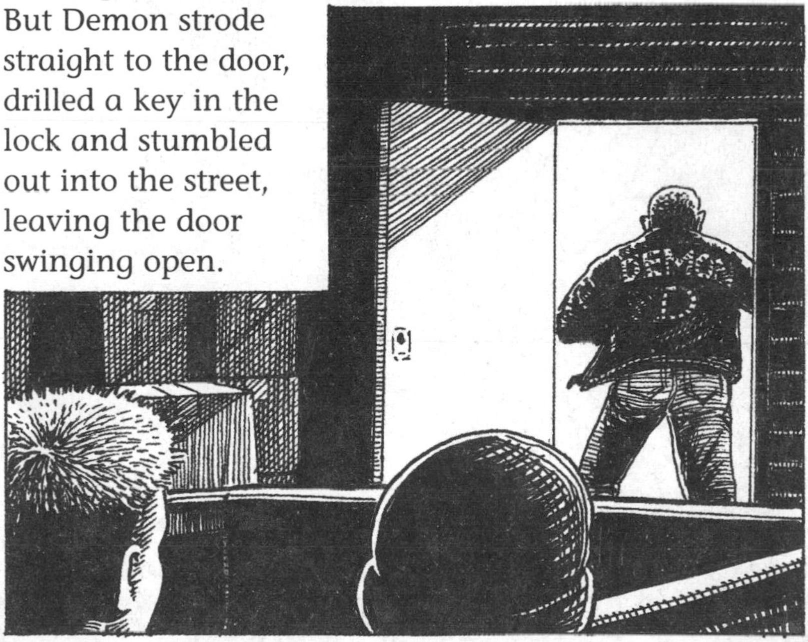

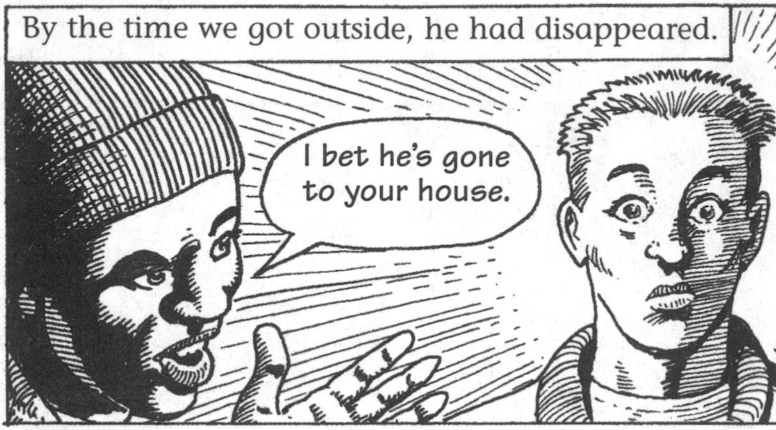
By the time we got outside, he had disappeared.
I bet he's gone to your house.

We sprinted all the way to the High Street and carried on up our road. But help was already at hand. A police van was outside our house!

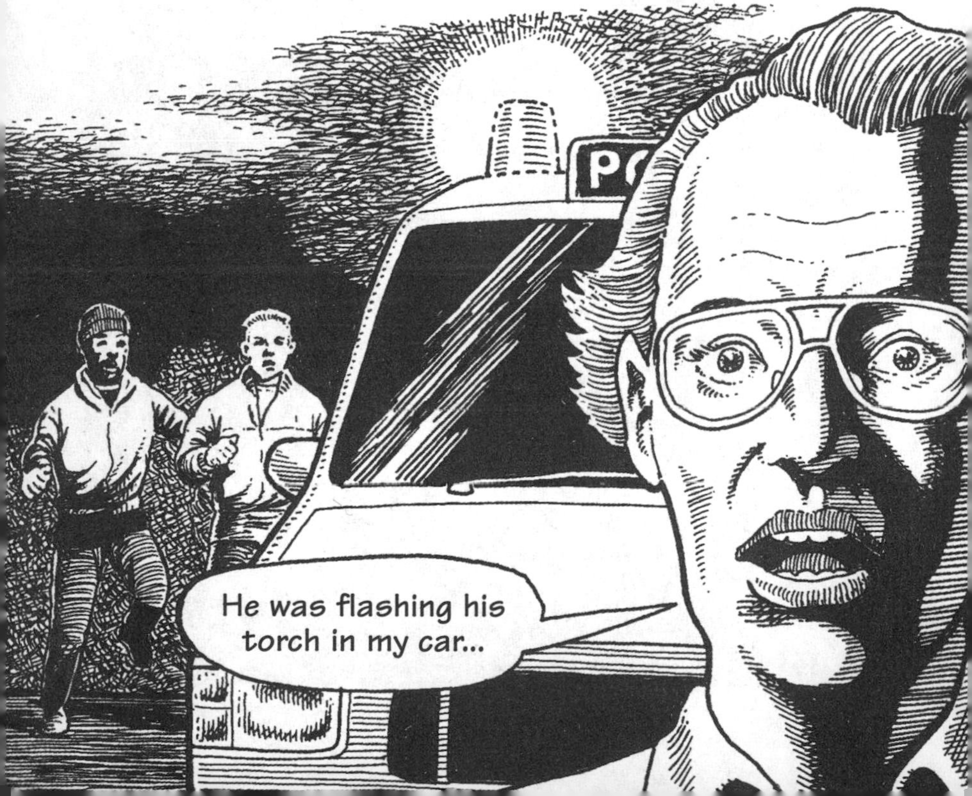
He was flashing his torch in my car...

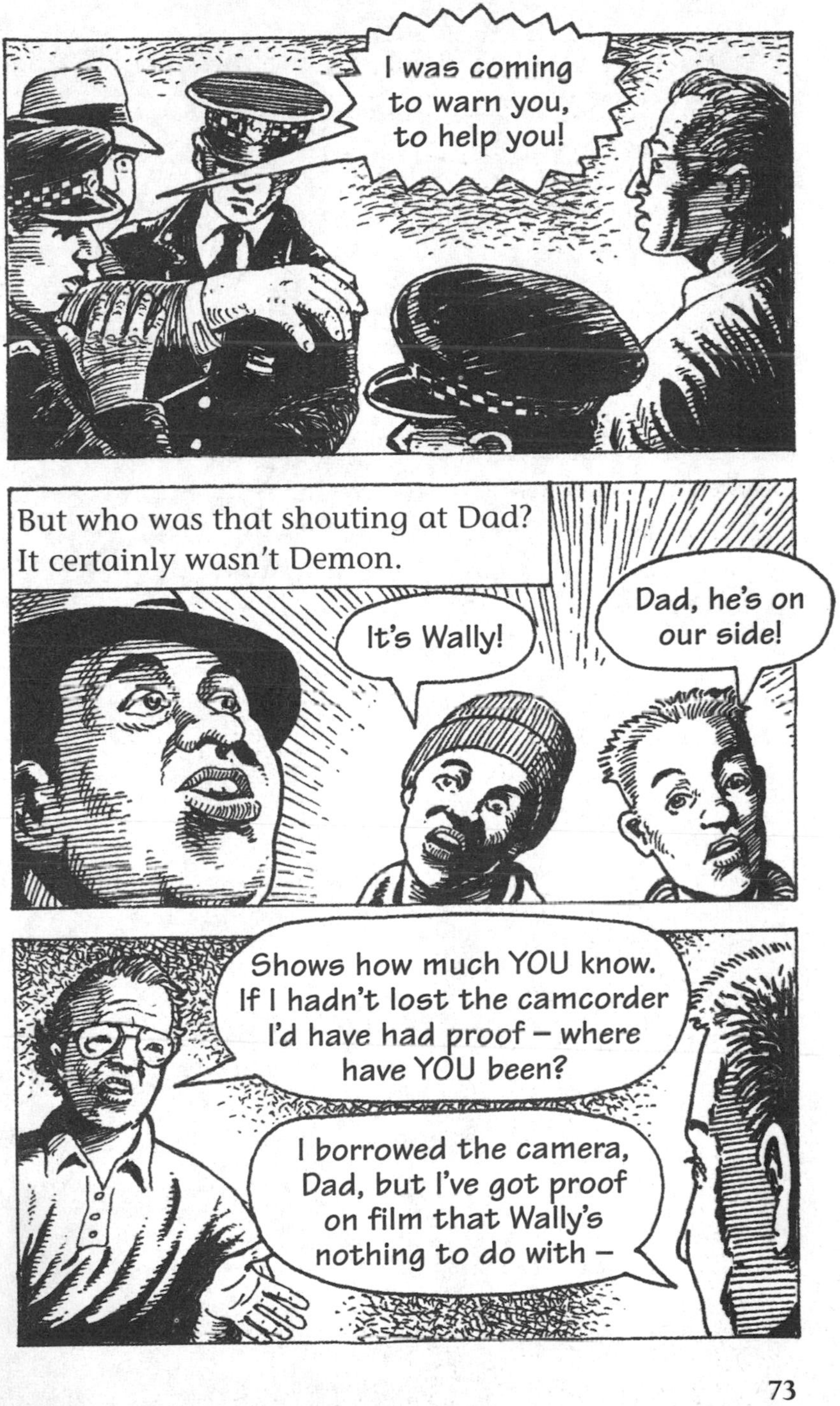
I was coming to warn you, to help you!
But who was that shouting at Dad? It certainly wasn't Demon.
It's Wally!
Dad, he's on our side!
Shows how much YOU know. If I hadn't lost the camcorder I'd have had proof – where have YOU been?
I borrowed the camera, Dad, but I've got proof on film that Wally's nothing to do with –

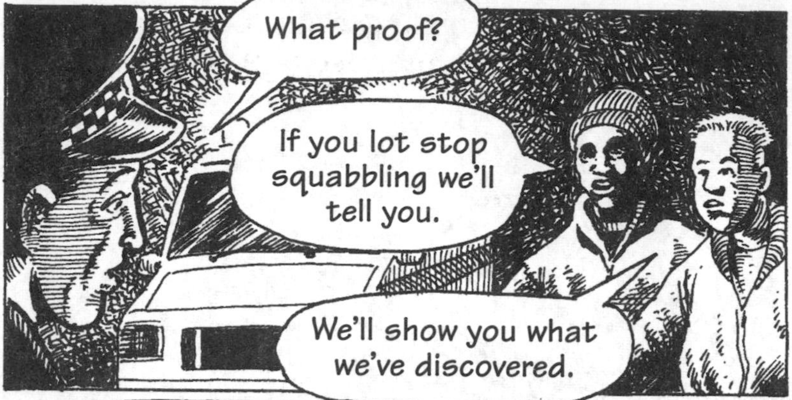
What proof?
If you lot stop squabbling we'll tell you.
We'll show you what we've discovered.

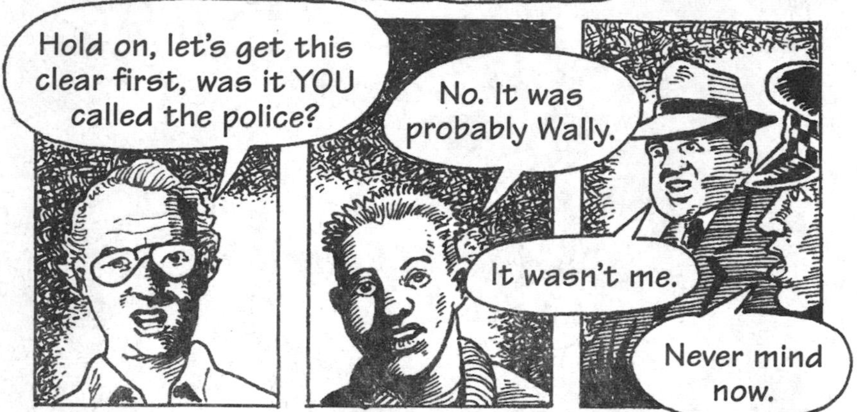
Hold on, let's get this clear first, was it YOU called the police?
No. It was probably Wally.
It wasn't me.
Never mind now.

We all piled in the police van and found our way back to the arches. The garage door was still open. But as we edged round the crates, into the inner vault, it all seemed dangerously quiet.

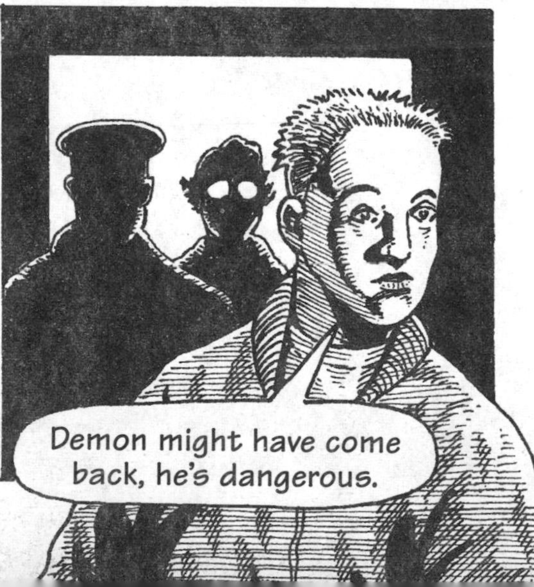
Demon might have come back, he's dangerous.

But the policemen were more concerned by all those video recorders. I'd left my video in there!

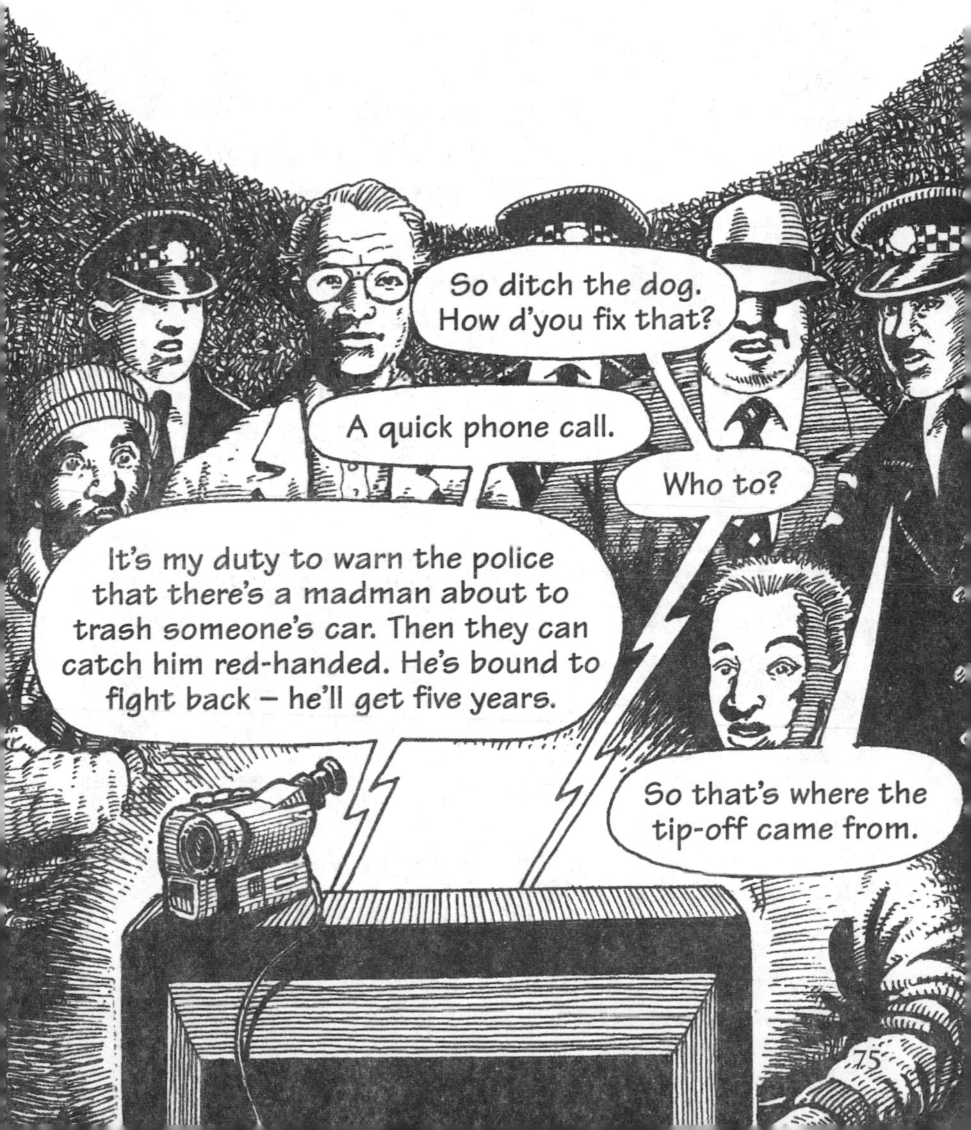
So ditch the dog. How d'you fix that?
A quick phone call.
Who to?
It's my duty to warn the police that there's a madman about to trash someone's car. Then they can catch him red-handed. He's bound to fight back – he'll get five years.
So that's where the tip-off came from.

Chapter nine

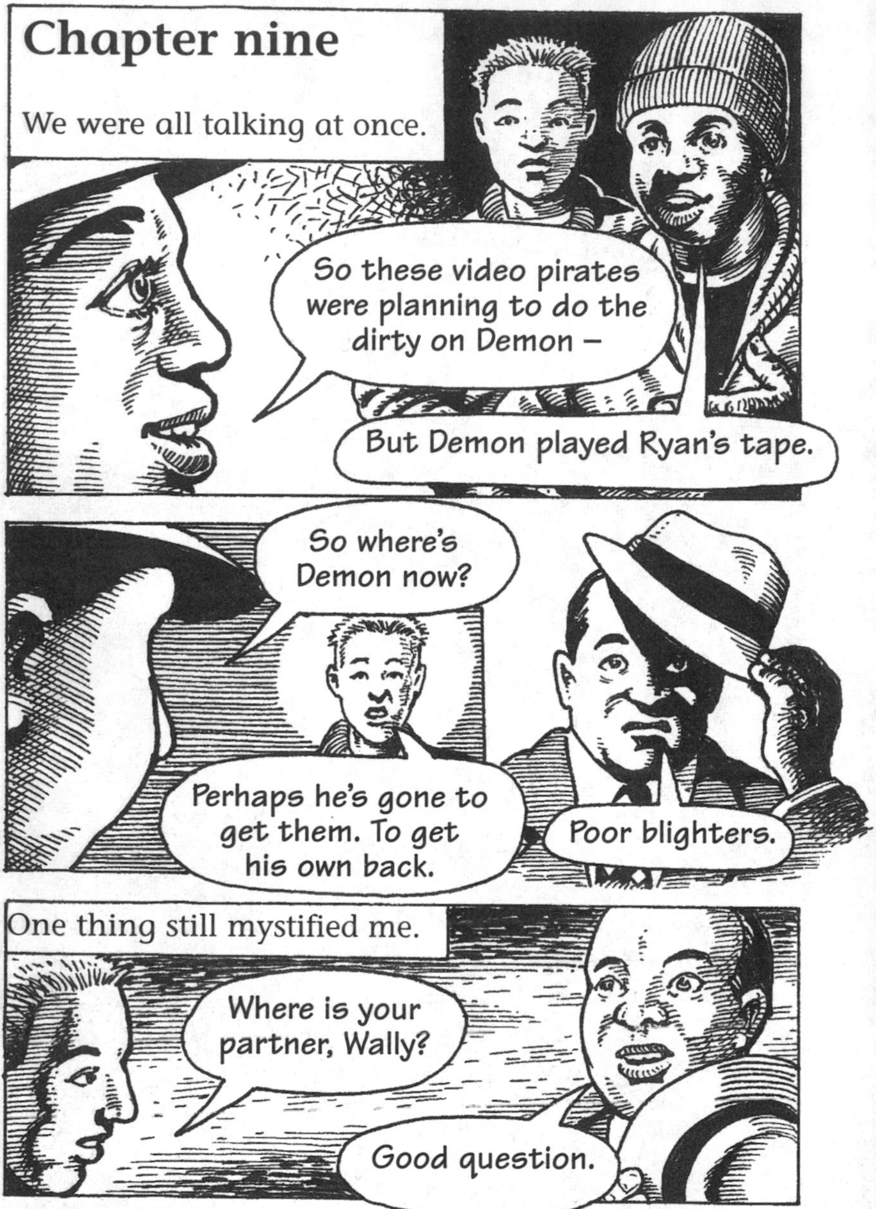
We were all talking at once.
So these video pirates were planning to do the dirty on Demon –
But Demon played Ryan's tape.
So where's Demon now?
Perhaps he's gone to get them. To get his own back.
Poor blighters.
One thing still mystified me.
Where is your partner, Wally?
Good question.

Before he could say more, Dad asked him to come home for supper. So we didn't hear his story until much later that evening.

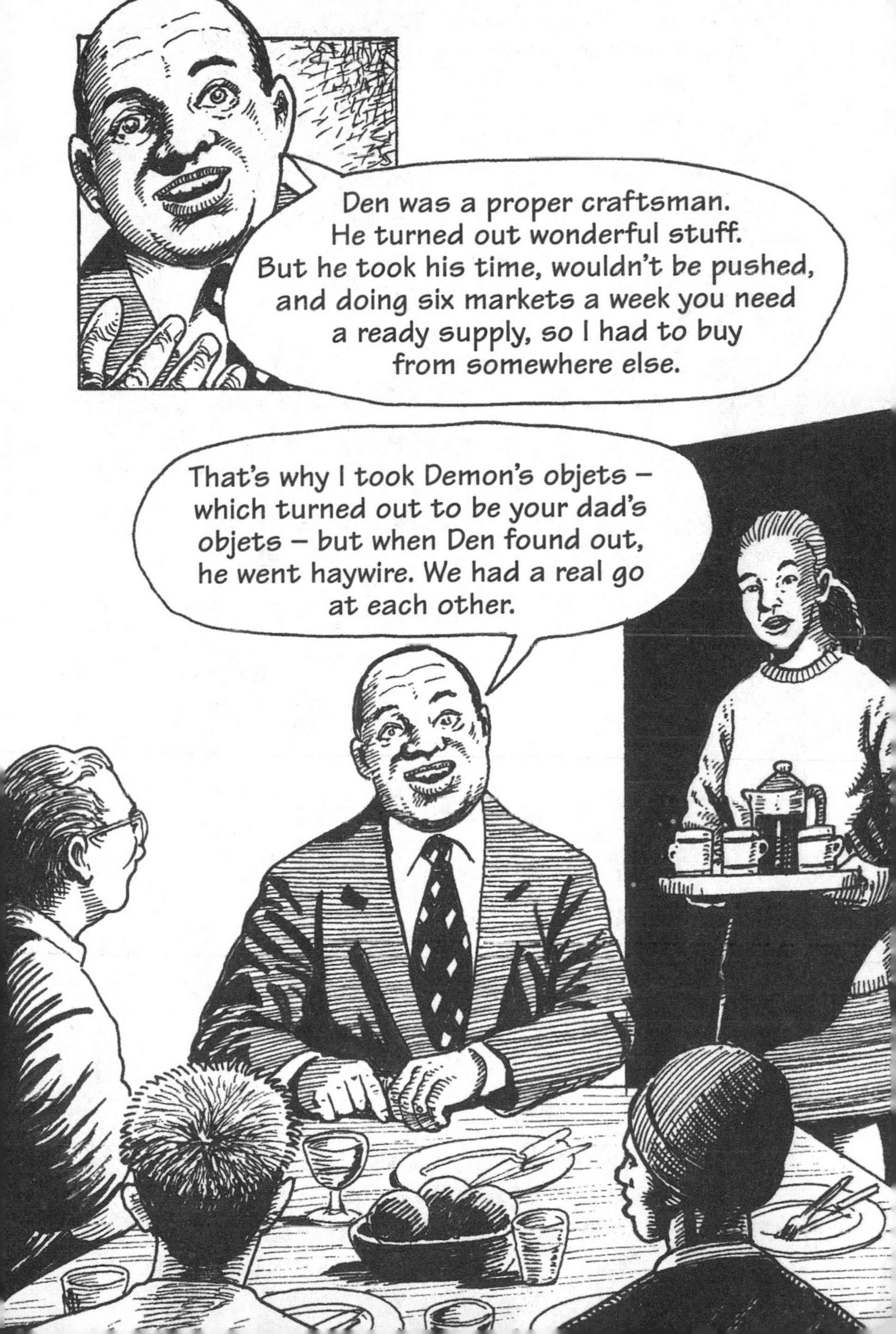
Den was a proper craftsman. He turned out wonderful stuff. But he took his time, wouldn't be pushed, and doing six markets a week you need a ready supply, so I had to buy from somewhere else.
That's why I took Demon's objets – which turned out to be your dad's objets – but when Den found out, he went haywire. We had a real go at each other.

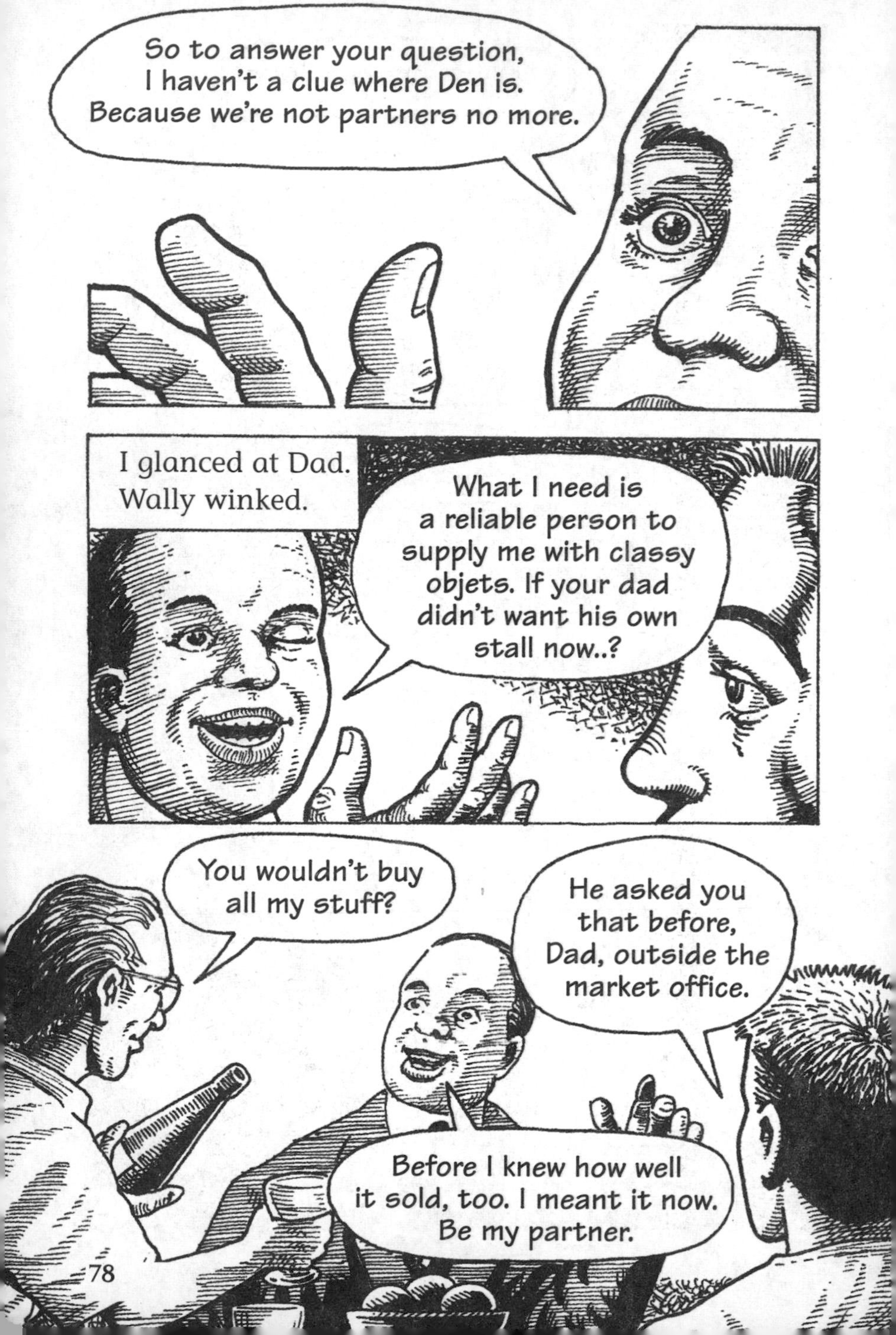
So to answer your question, I haven't a clue where Den is. Because we're not partners no more.
I glanced at Dad. Wally winked.
What I need is a reliable person to supply me with classy objets. If your dad didn't want his own stall now..?
You wouldn't buy all my stuff?
He asked you that before, Dad, outside the market office.
Before I knew how well it sold, too. I meant it now. Be my partner.

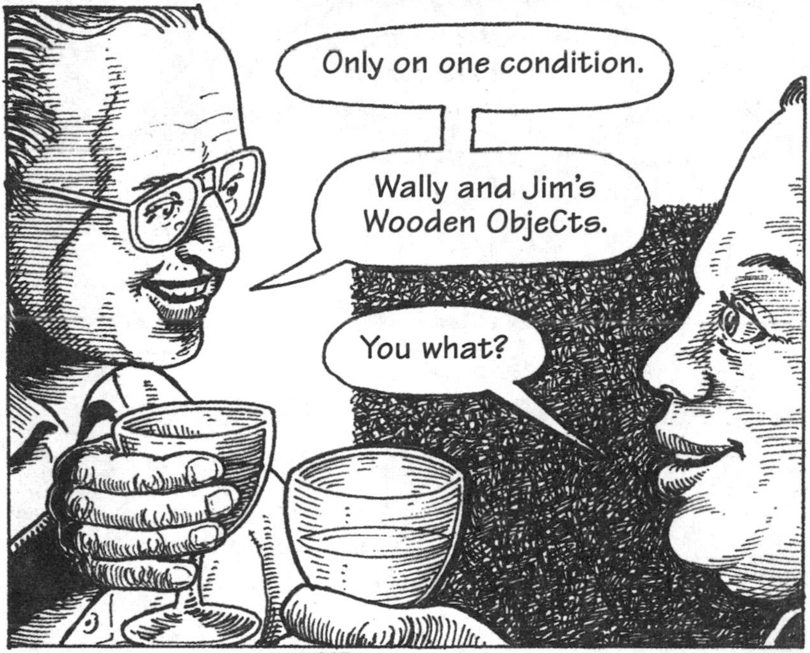
Only on one condition.
Wally and Jim's Wooden ObjeCts.
You what?

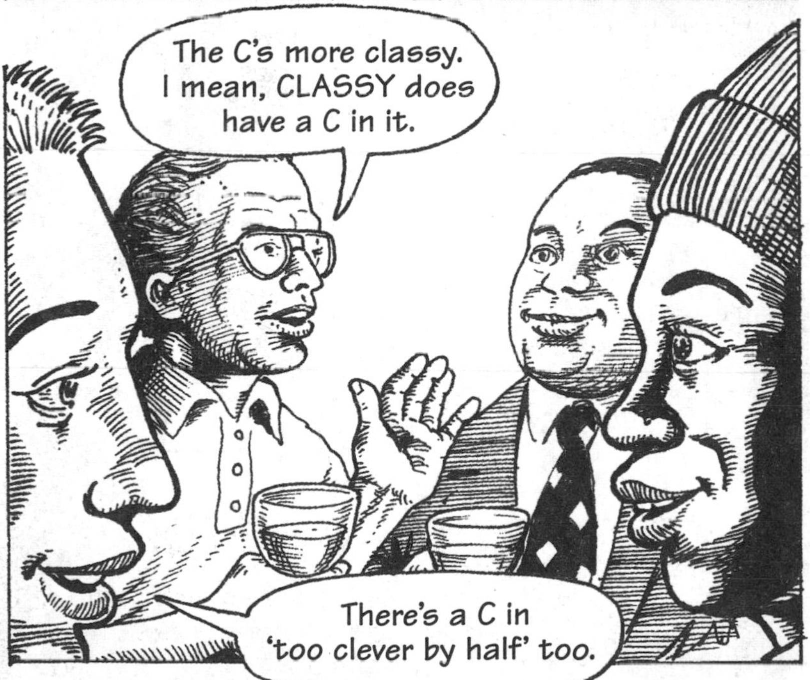
The C's more classy. I mean, CLASSY does have a C in it.
There's a C in 'too clever by half' too.

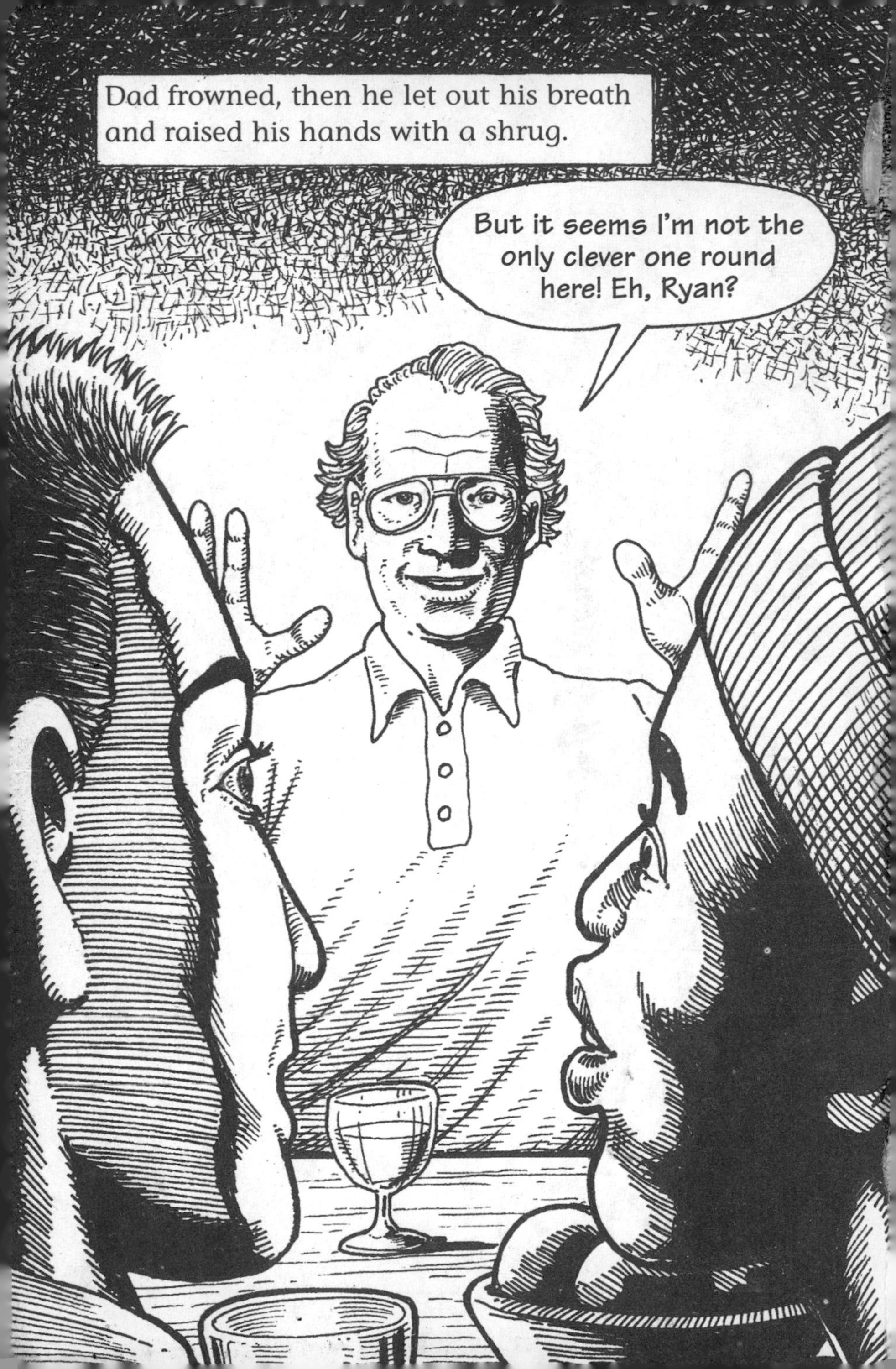
Dad frowned, then he let out his breath and raised his hands with a shrug.
But it seems I'm not the only clever one round here! Eh, Ryan?